HISTORY & GEOGRAPHY 700
Teacher's Guide

Author:

Teresa Busky, B.A., J.D.

Editor:

Alan Christopherson, M.S.

804 N. 2nd Ave. E.
Rock Rapids, IA 51246-1759

HISTORY & GEOGRAPHY 700

LIFEPAC® Overview

HISTORY & GEOGRAPHY SCOPE & SEQUENCE

	Your World (Grade 1)	U.S. History (Grade 2)	U.S. Geography and History (Grade 3)
Unit 1	I AM A SPECIAL PERSON • God made me • You are God's child • All about you • Using proper manners	LOOKING BACK Remembering last year Learning about early times The trail of the Native Americans Symbols and historic places	U.S. GEOGRAPHY AND HISTORY STUDY SKILLS • Map skills • Resources • Community
Unit 2	LET'S COMMUNICATE • Sounds people make • Sounds that communicate • Communicating without sound • Communicating with God	SETTLING THE NEW WORLD The first settlers Colonies of the new world War for Independence Symbols and historical places	NEW ENGLAND STATES • ME, NH, VT, MA, RI, and CT • New England geography • New England resources • New England community
Unit 3	I HAVE FEELINGS • I feel sad • I feel afraid • I feel happy • I have other feelings	A NEW GOVERNMENT FOR A NEW COUNTRY A study of government Creating a government Our government Symbols and historical places	MID-ATLANTIC STATES • NY, PA, NJ, DE, MD, and DC • Mid-Atlantic geography • Mid-Atlantic resources • Mid-Atlantic community
Unit 4	I LIVE IN A FAMILY • My mother and father • My brothers and sisters • My grandparents • What my family does	GOVERNMENT UNDER THE CONSTITUTION Article One – The Legislative Branch Article Two – The Executive Branch Article Three – The Judicial Branch The Bill of Rights – Symbols and historical places	SOUTHERN-ATLANTIC STATES • WV, VA, NC, SC, GA, and FL • Southern Atlantic geography • Southern Atlantic resources • Southern Atlantic community
Unit 5	YOU BELONG TO FAMILIES • Getting ready in the morning • Walking to school • The school family • The church family	OUR GOVERNMENT CLOSE TO HOME Our state governments Our local governments Citizens of the United States Symbols and historical places	SOUTHERN STATES • KY, TN, MS, LA, AL, OK, TX, and AR • Southern geography • Southern resources • Southern community
Unit 6	PLACES PEOPLE LIVE • Life on the farm • Life in the city • Life by the sea	WESTWARD – FROM THE ORIGINAL COLONIES The United States grows The Lewis and Clark Expedition The Old Southwest Symbols and historical places	GREAT LAKES STATES • OH, IN, IL, MI, WI, and MN • Great Lakes geography • Great Lakes resources • Great Lakes community
Unit 7	COMMUNITY HELPERS • Firefighters and police officers • Doctors • City workers • Teachers and ministers	SETTLING THE FRONTIER The Texas frontier Westward expansion Meet America's pioneers Symbols and historical places	MIDWESTERN STATES • ND, SD, NE, KS, MO, and IA • Midwestern geography • Midwestern resources • Midwestern community
Unit 8	I LOVE MY COUNTRY • America discovered • The Pilgrims • The United States begins • Respect for your country	EXPLORING AMERICA WITH MAPS Directions on a map Reading roads and symbols Natural features Symbols and historical places	MOUNTAIN STATES • MT, ID, WY, NV, UT, CO, AZ, and NM • Mountain geography • Mountain resources • Mountain community
Unit 9	I LIVE IN THE WORLD • The globe • Countries • Friends in Mexico • Friends in Japan	PAST, PRESENT, AND FUTURE MAPS City maps Building maps History of maps Symbols and historical places	PACIFIC STATES • WA, OR, CA, AK, and HI • Pacific geography • Pacific resources • Pacific community
Unit 10	THE WORLD AND YOU • You are special • Your family • Your school and church • Your world	REVIEW UNITED STATES HISTORY The United States begins Creating a government Mapping the United States	U.S. GEOGRAPHY AND HISTORY REVIEW • U.S. geographical features • Eastern U.S. review • Western U.S. review

HISTORY & GEOGRAPHY SCOPE & SEQUENCE

World Geography and Culture (Grade 4)	U.S. History (Grade 5)	Civilizations (Grade 6)	
OUR EARTH • The surface of the Earth • Early explorations of the Earth • Exploring from space • Exploring the oceans	A NEW WORLD • Exploration of America • The first colonies • Conflict with Britain • Birth of the United States	WORLD GEOGRAPHY • Latitude and longitude • Western and eastern hemispheres • The southern hemisphere • Political and cultural regions	Unit 1
SEAPORT CITIES • Sydney • Hong Kong • Istanbul • London	A NEW NATION • War for Independence • Life in America • A new form of government • The nation's early years	THE CRADLE OF CIVILIZATION • Mesopotamia • The land of Israel • The nation of Israel • Egypt	Unit 2
DESERT LANDS • What is a desert? • Where are the deserts? • How do people live in the desert?	A TIME OF TESTING • Louisiana Purchase • War of 1812 • Sectionalism • Improvements in trade and travel	THE CIVILIZATIONS OF GREECE AND ROME • Geography of the region • Beginning civilizations • Contributions to other civilizations • The influence of Christianity	Unit 3
GRASSLANDS • Grasslands of the world • Ukraine • Kenya • Argentina	A GROWING NATION • Andrew Jackson's influence • Texas and Oregon • Mexican War • The nation divides	LIFE IN THE MIDDLE AGES • The feudal system • Books and schools • The Crusades • Trade and architecture	Unit 4
TROPICAL RAINFORESTS • Facts about rainforests • Rainforests of the world • The Amazon rainforest • The Congo rainforest	A DIVIDED NATION • Civil War • Reconstruction • Gilded Age • The need for reform	SIX SOUTH AMERICAN COUNTRIES • Brazil • Colombia • Venezuela • Three Guianas	Unit 5
THE POLAR REGIONS • The polar regions: coldest places in the world • The Arctic polar region • The Antarctic polar region	A CHANGING NATION • Progressive reforms • Spanish-American War • World War I • Roaring Twenties	OTHER SOUTH AMERICAN COUNTRIES • Ecuador and Peru • Bolivia and Uruguay • Paraguay and Argentina • Chile	Unit 6
MOUNTAIN COUNTRIES • Peru — the Andes • The Incas and modern Peru • Nepal — the Himalayas • Switzerland — the Alps	DEPRESSION AND WAR • The Great Depression • War begins in Europe • War in Europe • War in the Pacific	AFRICA • Geography and cultures • Countries of northern Africa • Countries of central Africa • Countries of southern Africa	Unit 7
ISLAND COUNTRIES • Islands of the Earth • Cuba • Iceland • Japan	COLD WAR • Korean War and other crises • Vietnam War • Civil Rights movement • Upheaval in America	MODERN WESTERN EUROPE • The Renaissance • The Industrial Revolution • World War I • World War II	Unit 8
NORTH AMERICA • Geography • Lands, lakes, and rivers • Northern countries • Southern countries	INTO THE NEW MILLENNIUM • Watergate and détente • The fall of communism • The Persian Gulf • Issues of the new millennium	MODERN EASTERN EUROPE • Early government • Early churches • Early countries • Modern countries	Unit 9
OUR WORLD IN REVIEW • Europe and the explorers • Asia and Africa • Southern continents • North America and the North Pole	THE UNITED STATES OF AMERICA • Beginning America until 1830 • Stronger America 1830-1930 • 1930 to the end of the millennium • The new millennium	DEVELOPMENT OF OUR WORLD • Cradle of civilization • The Middle Ages • Modern Europe • South America and Africa	Unit 10

HISTORY & GEOGRAPHY SCOPE & SEQUENCE

	Anthropology, Sociology, Economics, and State History (Grade 7)	U.S. History (Grade 8)	Civics and World Geography (Grade 9)
Unit 1	WHAT IS HISTORY? • Definition and significance of history • Historians and the historical method • Views of history	EUROPE COMES TO AMERICA • Voyages of Columbus • Spanish exploration • Other exploration • The first colonies	HERITAGE OF THE UNITED STATES • American colonies • Acquisitions and annexations • Backgrounds to freedom • Backgrounds to society
Unit 2	WHAT IS GEOGRAPHY? • Classes of geography • Geography and relief of the Earth • Maps and the study of our world • Time zones	BRITISH AMERICA • English colonies • Government • Lifestyle • Wars with France	OUR NATIONAL GOVERNMENT • Ideals of national government • National government developed • Legislative and executive branches • Judicial branch
Unit 3	U.S. HISTORY AND GEOGRAPHY • Geography of the United States • Early history of the United States • Physical regions of the United States • Cultural regions of the United States	THE AMERICAN REVOLUTION • British control • Rebellion of the colonies • War for independence • Constitution	STATE AND LOCAL GOVERNMENT • Powers of state government • County government • Township government • City government
Unit 4	ANTHROPOLOGY • Understanding anthropology • The unity of man • The diversity of man • The culture of man	A FIRM FOUNDATION • Washington's presidency • Adams' administration • Jeffersonian Democracy • War of 1812	PLANNING A CAREER • Definition of a career • God's will concerning a career • Selecting a career • Preparation for a career
Unit 5	SOCIOLOGY — MAN IN GROUPS • Sociology defined • Historical development • Importance to Christians • Method of sociology	A GROWING NATION • Jacksonian Era • Northern border • Southern border • Industrial Revolution	CITIZENSHIP • Citizenship defined • Gaining citizenship • Rights of citizenship • Responsibilities of citizenship
Unit 6	U.S. ANTHROPOLOGY AND SOCIOLOGY • Cultural background of the United States • Native American cultures • Cultures from distant lands • Cultural and social interaction	THE CIVIL WAR • Division and secession • Civil War • Death of Lincoln • Reconstruction	THE EARTH AND MAN • Man inhabits the Earth • Man's home on the Earth • Man develops the Earth • The future of the Earth
Unit 7	ECONOMICS — RESOURCES AND NEED • Economics defined • Methods of the economist • Tools of the economist • An experiment in economy	GILDED AGE TO PROGRESSIVE ERA • Rise of industry • Wild West • America as a world power • Progressive era	REGIONS OF THE WORLD • A region defined • Geographic and climate regions • Cultural and political regions • Economic regions of Europe
Unit 8	POLITICAL SCIENCE • Definition of political science • Roots of Western thought • Modern political thinkers • Political theory	A WORLD IN CONFLICT • World War I • Great Depression • New Deal • World War II	MAN AND HIS ENVIRONMENT • The physical environment • Drug abuse • The social environment • Man's responsibilities
Unit 9	STATE ECONOMICS AND POLITICS • Background of state government • State government • State finance • State politics	COLD WAR AMERICA • Origins of the Cold War • Vietnam • Truman to Nixon • Ending of the Cold War	TOOLS OF THE GEOGRAPHER • The globe • Types of maps • Reading maps • The Earth in symbol form
Unit 10	SOCIAL SCIENCES REVIEW • History and geography • Anthropology • Sociology • Economics and politics	RECENT AMERICA AND REVIEW • Europe to independence • Colonies to the Civil War • Civil War to World War II • World War II through the Cold War	MAN IN A CHANGING WORLD • Development of the nation • Development of government • Development of the Earth • Solving problems

HISTORY & GEOGRAPHY SCOPE & SEQUENCE

World History (Grade 10)	American History (Grade 11)	Government and Economics (Grade 12)	
ANCIENT CIVILIZATIONS 1 • Origin of civilization • Early Egypt • Assyria and Babylonia • Persian civilization	**FOUNDATION OF THE REPUBLIC** • Democracy develops • Virginia • New England colonies • Middle and southern colonies	**INTERNATIONAL GOVERNMENTS** • Why have governments? • Types of governments • Governments in our world • Political thinkers	Unit 1
ANCIENT CIVILIZATIONS 2 • India • China • Greek civilization • Roman Empire	**DEVELOPMENT OF CONSTITUTIONAL GOVERNMENT** • Relations with England • The Revolutionary War • Articles of Confederation • Constitution of the United States	**UNITED STATES GOVERNMENT** • U.S. Constitution • Bill of Rights • Three branches of government • Legislative process	Unit 2
THE MEDIEVAL WORLD • Early Middle Ages • Middle Ages in transition • High Middle Ages	**NATIONAL EXPANSION** • A strong federal government • Revolution of 1800 • War of 1812 • Nationalism and sectionalism	**AMERICAN PARTY SYSTEM** • American party system • Development of political parties • Functions of political parties • Voting	Unit 3
RENAISSANCE AND REFORMATION • Changes in government and art • Changes in literature and thought • Advances in science • Reform within the church	**A NATION DIVIDED** • Issues of division • Division of land and people • Economics of slavery • Politics of slavery	**HISTORY OF GOVERNMENTS** • Primitive governments • Beginnings of democracy • Feudalism, theocracy, and democracy • Fascism and Nazism	Unit 4
GROWTH OF WORLD EMPIRES • England and France • Portugal and Spain • Austria and Germany • Italy and the Ottoman Empire	**A NATION DIVIDED AND UNITED** • Regionalism • The division • The Civil War • Reconstruction	**THE CHRISTIAN AND HIS GOVERNMENT** • Discrimination and the Christian • Christian attitudes • Public opinion and truth in politics • Politics and propaganda	Unit 5
THE AGE OF REVOLUTION • Factors leading to revolution • The English Revolution • The American Revolution • The French Revolution	**U.S. INVOLVEMENT AT HOME AND ABROAD** • Surge of industry • The industrial lifestyle • Isolationism • Involvement in conflict	**FREE ENTERPRISE** • Economics • Competition • Money through history • International finance and currency	Unit 6
THE INDUSTRIAL REVOLUTION • Sparks of preparation • Industrial Revolution in England • Industrial Revolution in America • Social changes of the revolution	**THE SEARCH FOR PEACE** • World War I and its aftermath • The Golden Twenties • The Great Depression • The New Deal	**BUSINESS AND YOU** • Running a business • Government and business • Banks and mergers • Deregulation and bankruptcy	Unit 7
TWO WORLD WARS • Mounting tension • World War I • Peace and power quests • World War II	**A NATION AT WAR** • Causes of the war • World War II • Korean conflict • Vietnam conflict	**THE STOCK MARKET** • How it started and works • Selecting stocks • Types of stocks • Tracking stocks	Unit 8
THE 20TH CENTURY AFTER 1945 • The Cold War • Korean War and Vietnam War • Collapse of the Soviet Union • The 20th century closes	**CONTEMPORARY AMERICA** • America in the 1960s • America in the 1970s • America in the 1980s and 1990s • International scene 1980s and 1990s	**BUDGET AND FINANCE** • Cash, credit, and checking • Buying a car • Grants, loans, and IRAs • Savings and eCash	Unit 9
ANCIENT TIMES TO THE 21ST CENTURY • Ancient civilizations • Medieval times • Renaissance and Reformation • Revolutions and Globalization	**UNITED STATES HISTORY** • Basis of democracy • The 1800s • Industrialization • Current history	**GEOGRAPHY** • Euro and International finance • U.S. geography • The global traveler • Neighbors, heroes, and the Holy Land	Unit 10

STRUCTURE OF THE LIFEPAC CURRICULUM

The LIFEPAC curriculum is conveniently structured to provide one Teacher's Guide containing teacher support material with answer keys and ten student worktexts for each subject at grade levels 2 through 12. The worktext format of the LIFEPACs allows the student to read the textual information and complete workbook activities all in the same booklet. The easy-to-follow LIFEPAC numbering system lists the grade as the first number(s) and the last two digits as the number of the series. For example, the Language Arts LIFEPAC at the 6th grade level, 5th book in the series would be LAN0605.

Each LIFEPAC is divided into three to five sections and begins with an introduction or overview of the booklet as well as a series of specific learning objectives to give a purpose to the study of the LIFEPAC. The introduction and objectives are followed by a vocabulary section which may be found at the beginning of each section at the lower levels or in the glossary at the high school level. Vocabulary words are used to develop word recognition and should not be confused with the spelling words introduced later in the LIFEPAC. The student should learn all vocabulary words before working the LIFEPAC sections to improve comprehension, retention, and reading skills.

Each activity or written assignment in grades 2 through 12 has a number for easy identification, such as 1.1. The first number corresponds to the LIFEPAC section and the number to the right of the decimal is the number of the activity.

Teacher checkpoints, which are essential to maintain quality learning, are found at various locations throughout the LIFEPAC.

The teacher should check 1) neatness of work and penmanship, 2) quality of understanding (tested with a short oral quiz), 3) thoroughness of answers (complete sentences and paragraphs, correct spelling, etc.), 4) completion of activities (no blank spaces), and 5) accuracy of answers as compared to the answer key (all answers correct).

The self test questions in grades 2 through 12 are also number coded for easy reference. For example, 2.015 means that this is the 15th question in the self test of Section 2. The first number corresponds to the LIFEPAC section, the zero indicates that it is a self test question, and the number to the right of the zero the question number.

The LIFEPAC test is packaged at the center of each LIFEPAC. It should be removed and put aside before giving the booklet to the student for study.

Answer and test keys in grades 2 through 12 have the same numbering system as the LIFEPACs. The student may be given access to the answer keys (not the test keys) under teacher supervision so that they can score their own work.

A thorough study of the Scope & Sequence by the teacher before instruction begins is essential to the success of the student. The teacher should become familiar with expected skill mastery and understand how these grade-level skills fit into the overall skill development of the curriculum. The teacher should also preview the objectives that appear at the beginning of each LIFEPAC for additional preparation and planning.

TEST SCORING AND GRADING

Answer keys and test keys give examples of correct answers. They convey the idea, but the student may use many ways to express a correct answer. The teacher should check for the essence of the answer, not for the exact wording. Many questions are high level and require thinking and creativity on the part of the student. Each answer should be scored based on whether or not the main idea written by the student matches the model example. "Any Order" or "Either Order" in a key indicates that no particular order is necessary to be correct.

Most self tests and LIFEPAC tests at the lower elementary levels are scored at 1 point per answer; however, the upper levels may have a point system awarding 2 to 5 points for various answers or questions. Further, the total test points will vary; they may not always equal 100 points. They may be 78, 85, 100, 105, etc.

Example 1

Example 2

A score box similar to ex. 1 above is located at the end of each self test and on the front of the LIFEPAC test. The bottom score, 72, represents the total number of points possible on the test. The upper score, 58, represents the number of points your student will need to receive an 80% or passing grade. If you wish to establish the exact percentage that your student has achieved, find the total points of their correct answers and divide it by the bottom number (in this case 72). For example, if your student has a point total of 65, divide 65 by 72 for a grade of 90%. Referring to ex. 2, on a test with a total of 105 possible points, the student would have to receive a minimum of 84 correct points for an 80% or passing grade. If your student has received 93 points, simply divide the 93 by 105 for a percentage grade of 89%. Students who receive a score below 80% should review the LIFEPAC and retest using the appropriate Alternate Test found in the Teacher's Guide.

The following is a guideline to assign letter grades for completed LIFEPACs based on a maximum total score of 100 points.

Example:

LIFEPAC Test	=	60% of the Total Score (or percent grade)
Self Test	=	25% of the Total Score (average percent of self tests)
Reports	=	10% or 10* points per LIFEPAC
Oral Work	=	5% or 5* points per LIFEPAC

*Determined by the teacher's subjective evaluation of the student's daily work.

Example:

LIFEPAC Test Score	=	92%	92 × .60	=	55 points
Self Test Average	=	90%	90 × .25	=	23 points
Reports				=	8 points
Oral Work				=	4 points
TOTAL POINTS				=	90 points

Grade Scale based on point system:

100 – 94	=	A
93 – 86	=	B
85 – 77	=	C
76 – 70	=	D
Below 70	=	F

TEACHER GUIDANCE AND STUDYING TECHNIQUES

LIFEPAC activities are written to check the level of understanding of the preceding text. The student may look back to the text as necessary to complete these activities; however, a student should never attempt to do the activities without reading (studying) the text first. Self tests and LIFEPAC tests are never open book tests.

Language arts activities (skill integration) often appear within other subject curriculum. The purpose is to give the student an opportunity to test their skill mastery outside of the context in which it was presented.

Writing complete answers (paragraphs) to some questions is an integral part of the LIFEPAC curriculum in all subjects. This builds communication and organization skills, increases understanding and retention of ideas, and helps enforce good penmanship. Complete sentences should be encouraged for this type of activity. Obviously, single words or phrases do not meet the intent of the activity, since multiple lines are given for the response.

Review is essential to student success. Time invested in review where review is suggested will be time saved in correcting errors later. Self tests, unlike the section activities, are closed book. This procedure helps to identify weaknesses before they become too great to overcome. Certain objectives from self tests are cumulative and test previous sections; therefore, good preparation for a self test must include all material studied up to that testing point.

The following procedure checklist has been found to be successful in developing good study habits in the LIFEPAC curriculum.

1. Read the introduction and Table of Contents.
2. Read the objectives.
3. Recite and study the entire vocabulary (glossary) list.
4. Study each section as follows:
   a. Read the introduction and study the section objectives.
   b. Read all the text for the entire section, but answer none of the activities.
   c. Return to the beginning of the section and memorize each vocabulary word and definition.
   d. Reread the section, complete the activities, check the answers with the answer key, correct all errors, and have the teacher check.
   e. Read the self test but do not answer the questions.
   f. Go to the beginning of the first section and reread the text and answers to the activities up to the self test you have not yet done.
   g. Answer the questions to the self test without looking back.
   h. Have the self test checked by the teacher.
   i. Correct the self test and have the teacher check the corrections.
   j. Repeat steps a–i for each section.
5. Use the **SQ3R** method to prepare for the LIFEPAC test.
   > **S**can the whole LIFEPAC.
   > **Q**uestion yourself on the objectives.
   > **R**ead the whole LIFEPAC again.
   > **R**ecite through an oral examination.
   > **R**eview weak areas.
6. Take the LIFEPAC test as a closed book test.
7. LIFEPAC tests are administered and scored under direct teacher supervision. Students who receive scores below 80% should review the LIFEPAC using the **SQ3R** study method and take the Alternate Test located in the Teacher's Guide. The final test grade may be the grade on the Alternate Test or an average of the grades from the original LIFEPAC test and the Alternate Test.

GOAL SETTING AND SCHEDULES

Each school must develop its own schedule, because no single set of procedures will fit every situation. The following is an example of a daily schedule that includes the five LIFEPAC subjects as well as time slotted for special activities.

Possible Daily Schedule

8:15	–	8:25	Pledges, prayer, songs, devotions, etc.
8:25	–	9:10	Bible
9:10	–	9:55	Language Arts
9:55	–	10:15	Recess (juice break)
10:15	–	11:00	Math
11:00	–	11:45	History & Geography
11:45	–	12:30	Lunch, recess, quiet time
12:30	–	1:15	Science
1:15	–		Drill, remedial work, enrichment*

*Enrichment: *Computer time, physical education, field trips, fun reading, games and puzzles, family business, hobbies, resource persons, guests, crafts, creative work, electives, music appreciation, projects.*

Basically, two factors need to be considered when assigning work to a student in the LIFEPAC curriculum.

The first is time. An average of 45 minutes should be devoted to each subject, each day. Remember, this is only an average. Because of extenuating circumstances, a student may spend only 15 minutes on a subject one day and the next day spend 90 minutes on the same subject.

The second factor is the number of pages to be worked in each subject. A single LIFEPAC is designed to take three to four weeks to complete. Allowing about three to four days for LIFEPAC introduction, review, and tests, the student has approximately 15 days to complete the LIFEPAC pages. Simply take the number of pages in the LIFEPAC, divide it by 15 and you will have the number of pages that must be completed on a daily basis to keep the student on schedule. For example, a LIFEPAC containing 45 pages will require three completed pages per day. Again, this is only an average. While working a 45-page LIFEPAC, the student may complete only one page the first day if the text has a lot of activities or reports, but go on to complete five pages the next day.

Long-range planning requires some organization. Because the traditional school year originates in the early fall of one year and continues to late spring of the following year, a calendar should be devised that covers this period of time. Approximate beginning and completion dates can be noted on the calendar as well as special occasions such as holidays, vacations and birthdays. Since each LIFEPAC takes three to four weeks or 18 days to complete, it should take about 180 school days to finish a set of ten LIFEPACs. Starting at the beginning school date, mark off 18 school days on the calendar and that will become the targeted completion date for the first LIFEPAC. Continue marking the calendar until you have established dates for the remaining nine LIFEPACs making adjustments for previously noted holidays and vacations. If all five subjects are being used, the ten established target dates should be the same for the LIFEPACs in each subject.

TEACHING SUPPLEMENTS

The sample weekly lesson plan and student grading sheet forms are included in this section as teacher support materials and may be duplicated at the convenience of the teacher.

The student grading sheet is provided for those who desire to follow the suggested guidelines for assignment of letter grades as previously discussed. The student's self test scores should be posted as percentage grades. When the LIFEPAC is completed the teacher should average the self test grades, multiply the average by .25 and post the points in the box marked self test points. The LIFEPAC percentage grade should be multiplied by .60 and posted. Next, the teacher should award and post points for written reports and oral work. A report may be any type of written work assigned to the student whether it is a LIFEPAC or additional learning activity. Oral work includes the student's ability to respond orally to questions which may or may not be related to LIFEPAC activities or any type of oral report assigned by the teacher. The points may then be totaled and a final grade entered along with the date that the LIFEPAC was completed.

The Student Record Book, which was specifically designed for use with the Alpha Omega curriculum, provides space to record weekly progress for one student over a nine-week period as well as a place to post self test and LIFEPAC scores. The Student Record Books are available through the current Alpha Omega catalog; however, unlike the enclosed forms these books are not for duplication and should be purchased in sets of four to cover a full academic year.

WEEKLY LESSON PLANNER

Week of:

	Subject	Subject	Subject	Subject
Monday				
Tuesday	Subject	Subject	Subject	Subject
Wednesday	Subject	Subject	Subject	Subject
Thursday	Subject	Subject	Subject	Subject
Friday	Subject	Subject	Subject	Subject

WEEKLY LESSON PLANNER

Week of:

	Subject	Subject	Subject	Subject
Monday				
Tuesday	Subject	Subject	Subject	Subject
Wednesday	Subject	Subject	Subject	Subject
Thursday	Subject	Subject	Subject	Subject
Friday	Subject	Subject	Subject	Subject

Student Name _____   Year _____

Bible

LP	Self Test Scores by Sections 1	2	3	4	5	Self Test Points	LIFEPAC Test	Oral Points	Report Points	Final Grade	Date
01											
02											
03											
04											
05											
06											
07											
08											
09											
10											

History & Geography

LP	Self Test Scores by Sections 1	2	3	4	5	Self Test Points	LIFEPAC Test	Oral Points	Report Points	Final Grade	Date
01											
02											
03											
04											
05											
06											
07											
08											
09											
10											

Language Arts

LP	Self Test Scores by Sections 1	2	3	4	5	Self Test Points	LIFEPAC Test	Oral Points	Report Points	Final Grade	Date
01											
02											
03											
04											
05											
06											
07											
08											
09											
10											

Student Name _____   Year _____

Math

LP	Self Test Scores by Sections 1	2	3	4	5	Self Test Points	LIFEPAC Test	Oral Points	Report Points	Final Grade	Date
01											
02											
03											
04											
05											
06											
07											
08											
09											
10											

Science

LP	Self Test Scores by Sections 1	2	3	4	5	Self Test Points	LIFEPAC Test	Oral Points	Report Points	Final Grade	Date
01											
02											
03											
04											
05											
06											
07											
08											
09											
10											

Spelling/Electives

LP	Self Test Scores by Sections 1	2	3	4	5	Self Test Points	LIFEPAC Test	Oral Points	Report Points	Final Grade	Date
01											
02											
03											
04											
05											
06											
07											
08											
09											
10											

INSTRUCTIONS FOR HISTORY & GEOGRAPHY

The LIFEPAC curriculum from grades 2 through 12 is structured so that the daily instructional material is written directly into the LIFEPACs. The student is encouraged to read and follow this instructional material in order to develop independent study habits. The teacher should introduce the LIFEPAC to the student, set a required completion schedule, complete teacher checks, be available for questions regarding both content and procedures, administer and grade tests, and develop additional learning activities as desired. Teachers working with several students may schedule their time so that students are assigned to a quiet work activity when it is necessary to spend instructional time with one particular student.

The Teacher Notes section of the Teacher's Guide lists the required or suggested materials for the LIFEPACs and provides additional learning activities for the students. The materials section refers only to LIFEPAC materials and does not include materials which may be needed for the additional activities. Additional learning activities provide a change from the daily school routine, encourage the student's interest in learning and may be used as a reward for good study habits.

HISTORY & GEOGRAPHY 701

Unit 1: What is History?

TEACHER NOTES

MATERIALS NEEDED FOR LIFEPAC	
Required	Suggested
None	• the Bible, King James Version • Bible dictionary • *Halley's Bible Handbook* • reference books or online sources

ADDITIONAL LEARNING ACTIVITIES

Section 1: The Definition and Significance of History

1. Have students define the word, *history*. Ask students, does history have any effect on your life?

2. Discuss as a class: Would you rather live in the "good old days" or today?

3. Discuss some things we might like to have back from the "good old days" (examples: family life, honesty, less crime, neighborliness).
   Discuss some things we might *not* want back (diseases like smallpox and polio, segregation, poor transportation).

4. Discuss this concept: Some day, people will refer to today as the good old days. What are some of the things you think they will remember as being good?

5. Ask the class these questions: How would Christ view our times? Of what would He approve? Of what would He disapprove?

6. Bring an old newspaper, magazine, or yearbook to school. Compare how styles have changed.

7. Instruct students to locate, in an encyclopedia or online, the biography of one or two famous historians, to prepare for the following task:
   What qualities made them great? List and discuss these qualities. Do you or anyone in your group possess any of these qualities?

8. Assign students to write one or two paragraphs on which period in history they would have liked to live in. Ask, why did you pick that time?

9. Have students describe a current event as though they were a historian writing about it twenty years from now.

Section 2: Historians and the Historical Method

1. Discuss these questions with your class.

   a. Could the writers of Scripture be called historians?

   b. Do you think we have learned from the mistakes of the past?

   c. Is the Bible history?

2. Instruct students to compare a news article with a historical article by providing them with the following questions: How does the historian's method differ from the journalist's? Are there any similarities?

3. Arrange a visit a museum in your town. Have students look for some of the items a historian would use in their writings.

4. Assign the following project to accompany the museum visit: Select an item that particularly interests you. Do some research on it and write a 250-word paper.

5. Arrange a visit to a library so students can find information on archaeological finds, particularly in Biblical areas. You may also have students search for recent discoveries online.

6. Have students read a diary of a well-known person and write some facts that a historian could use—customs of the times, current events, and so forth.

7. Tell students to pretend to be a historical figure and write a diary that would cover a typical day in this person's life.

Section 3: Two Views of History

1. Discuss these questions with your class.

    a. Is it possible that the cyclical view of history is partly true, and that there is a time of extreme wickedness and immorality, then a time of spiritual awakening, and so on? This cyclical view could also be part of the linear view of history.

    b. Where did Moses get the material to write the Pentateuch?

2. Invite an archaeologist, preferably a Christian, to speak to your class.

3. Have a debate—the linear view of history versus the cyclical view. This activity will involve some research on the early Greeks and their beliefs.

4. Have the class follow a current event and assume the role of a historian. Arrange a visit your state legislature in session, your city council, or perhaps a court trial, if possible. Have each student take notes and write a short "historical" report. If a visit is not possible, you can have them obtain similar information from online sources. To wrap up the assignment, have students compare reports and discuss the following: Do the facts agree, or did some students interpret information differently? This activity will help point out the problems historians face.

5. Discuss the following: Are there people living today who still have beliefs like the Greeks, that man can cope with his environment, solve some of his problems, and that there is no eternal significance to what he does? Have students write a paragraph stating the Christian's view. (Can man solve his own problems?)

6. Assign students to write a 100- to 200-word report of Nebuchadnezzar's dream that Daniel interpreted. Students can use a Bible dictionary or reliable online sources for research.

Administer the LIFEPAC Test

The test is to be administered in one session. Give no help except with directions.
Evaluate the tests and review areas where the students have done poorly.
Review the pages and activities that stress the concepts tested.
If necessary, administer the Alternate LIFEPAC Test.

ANSWER KEYS

SECTION 1

1.1	b
1.2	d
1.3	a
1.4	f
1.5	e
1.6	c
1.7	The definition of history we will use is that history is the known story of people and our relationship with God, other people, and our environment.
1.8	no
1.9	definition
1.10	Exodus 20:1-11
1.11	Exodus 20:11-23:9
1.12	Genesis 1:28; Exodus 23:10-12
1.13	Any order:
	a. Do not take the name of the Lord in vain
	b. Have no other gods before God
	c. Do not make idols
	d. Remember the Sabbath day and keep it holy
1.14	Any order:
	a. Honor your mother and father
	b. Do not kill
	c. Do not steal
	d. Do not commit adultery
	e. Do not covet what others have
	f. Do not tell a lie about someone
1.15	Any order:
	a. replenish it
	b. subdue it
	c. have dominion over every living thing on earth
	d. every seventh year let the land rest
1.16	Any five:
	a. political
	b. social
	c. cultural
	d. racial
	e. religious
	or technological economic
1.17	Either order:
	a. order
	b. significance
1.18	Either order:
	a. present
	b. future

1.19	a. perils
	b. opportunities
1.20	a. last
	b. value and dependability
1.21	Egyptians
1.22	Hebrews
1.23	Babylonians
1.24	Phoenicians
1.25	Hebrews
1.26	Phoenicians
1.27	Babylonians
1.28	Egyptians
1.29	Egyptians
1.30	Example:
	If we know the successes of the past we can use them to make the present a "success." The contributions make our lives better today, give us "necessities of life"—a calendar, irrigation, astronomy.
1.31	Human
1.32	sinful
1.33	Creator
1.34	Ecclesiastes 1:9
1.35	born again
	or saved
1.36	all
1.37	heirs
1.38	Any order:
	a. knowledge
	b. institutions
	c. ideas
1.39	river
1.40	continuity
1.41	God
1.42	Either order:
	a. B.C.
	b. A.D.
1.43	Any order:
	a. ancient
	b. medieval
	c. modern
1.44	Either order:
	a. materials
	b. tools
1.45	*BC means* Before Christ (the time before Christ)
	BCE means Before the Common Era
1.46	*AD means* in the year of our Lord
	CE means Common Era

1.47   Ancient
1.48   Medieval
1.49   Modern
1.50   a. world
           b. flesh
           c. Satan
1.51   man
1.52   nature
1.53   fellowship
1.54   Babel
1.55   humanism
1.56   Any order:
           a. Gird loins with the truth
           b. Breastplate of righteousness
           c. Feet shod with the preparation of the gospel of peace
           d. Shield of faith
           e. Helmet of salvation
           f. Sword of the Spirit
1.57   spiritual vacuum
1.58   a. God's
           b. men
           c. God
           d. nature
1.59   "And we know that all things work together for good to them that love God, to them who are the called according to His purpose."

SELF TEST 1

1.01   true
1.02   true
1.03   true
1.04   true
1.05   false
1.06   false
1.07   true
1.08   God
1.09   fellowship
1.010   in the year of our Lord
1.011   people
            or men
1.012   Before Christ (the time before Christ)
1.013   a. sinful
            b. born again
            or saved
1.014   God
1.015   Babel
1.016   a. Creation
            b. 500
1.017   a. 500
            b. 1500
1.018   a. 1500
            b. present
1.019   Phoenicians
1.020   Babylonians and Egyptians
1.021   Egyptians
1.022   Hebrews
1.023   Egyptians
1.024   Egyptians
1.025   Phoenicians
1.026   Babylonians
1.027   Hebrews
1.028   a. Gird loins with the truth
            b. Breastplate of righteousness
            c. Feet shod with the preparation of the gospel of peace
            d. Shield of faith
            e. Helmet of salvation
            f. Sword of the Spirit

SECTION 2

2.1   ACROSS
1. historical geology
2. historiography
3. archaeologist
4. linguist

DOWN
1. statistician
2. numismatist
3. epigrapher

2.2   historians
2.3   imagination
2.4   false
2.5   true
2.6   a. honest
b. versatile
c. imaginative
d. judgmental
e. moral
f. tenacious
g. unprejudiced
h. patient
i. accurate
2.7   The practice of writing history.
2.8   One who studies history from the remains of human cultures.
2.9   One who interprets ancient inscriptions (writings).
2.10   One who studies coins, medals, or paper money.
2.11   One skilled in collecting and arranging data.
2.12   One who can speak several languages.
2.13   c
2.14   e
2.15   g
2.16   k
2.17   i
2.18   b
2.19   j
2.20   h
2.21   f
2.22   d
2.23   a
2.24   Either order:
a. primary
b. secondary
2.25   primary
2.26   secondary

2.27   Any order:
a. libraries
b. archives
c. museums
d. ruins
2.28   a. libraries
b. primary
2.29   Any order:
a. material remains
b. oral traditions
c. pictorial data
d. written records
2.30   a. archaeological remains
b. written
2.31   historical geology
2.32   a. salinity
b. sedimentation
c. decay
2.33   false
2.34   none
2.35   impossible
2.36   a. condition
b. constant
2.37   analyze
2.38   quality
2.39   a. man
b. Lord
2.40   a. collection
b. classification
c. analysis
d. interpretation
e. synthesis

SELF TEST 2

2.01 a. salinity
        b. sedimentation
        c. radioactive
2.02 a. primary
        b. secondary
2.03 primary
2.04 a. archaeological remains
        b. written records
2.05 geology
2.06 a. outward appearance
        b. heart
2.07 the environment
        or nature
2.08 Historiography
2.09 God
2.010 secondary
2.011 God
2.012 g
2.013 e
2.014 a
2.015 i
2.016 c
2.017 f
2.018 h
2.019 b
2.020 a. collect the data
        b. classify and date the data
        c. analyze the data
        d. interpret the data
        e. synthesize the data
2.021 a. Creation
        b. 500
2.022 a. 500
        b. 1500
2.023 a. 1500
        b. the present
2.024 Before Christ

SECTION 3

3.1 b
3.2 d
3.3 a
3.4 c
3.5 Hebrew civilization
3.6 Greek
3.7 incomplete
3.8 Linear
3.9 a. purpose
      b. significance
3.10 God
3.11 a. creation
       b. judgment
3.12 God
3.13 Word

SELF TEST 3

3.01   Hebrew civilization
3.02   incomplete
3.03   archaeologist
3.04   humanism
3.05   numismatist
3.06   epigrapher
3.07   historian
3.08   statistician
3.09   a. creation
        b. judgment
3.010 a. archaeological remains
        b. written
3.011 linear
3.012 cyclical
3.013 God
3.014 source
3.015 none
3.016 a. collect
        b. classify, date
        c. analyze
        d. interpret
        e. synthesize
3.017 h
3.018 d
3.019 j
3.020 b
3.021 g
3.022 a
3.023 c
3.024 e
3.025 f
3.026 k
3.027 m

LIFEPAC TEST

1. e
2. i
3. d *or* e
4. h
5. d
6. b
7. a
8. c
9. f
10. true
11. false
12. true
13. true
14. false
15. true
16. true
17. true
18. false
19. true
20. true
21. false
22. b
23. d
24. f
25. h
26. j
27. i
28. g
29. e
30. c
31. a
32. a
33. c
34. a, d
35. b
36. c
37. d
38. b
39. a
40. b
41.
   a. patient
   b. imaginative
   c. good judgment
   d. unprejudiced
   e. versatile
   f. tenacious
   g. honest
   h. accurate
   i. moral

ALTERNATE LIFEPAC TEST

1.
   a. God
   b. mankind
   c. environmental
2. Any three:
   a. political
   b. social
   c. economic
   or cultural
       technological
       racial
       religious
3. born again
4. Any order:
   a. ancient
   b. medieval
   c. modern
5. armor
6. Samaria
7. Either order:
   a. primary
   b. secondary
8. Any two:
   a. material remains
   b. oral traditions
   or pictorial data
       written records
9. Any two:
   a. salinity (saltiness) of the sea
   b. sedimentation
   or radioactive methods
10. c
11. b
12. a
13. d
14. d
15. d
16. b
17. c
18. d
19. b
20. c
21. a
22. h
23. b
24. g
25. f
26. d
27. Any order:
   a. collecting data
   b. classifying data
   c. analyzing data
   d. interpreting data
   e. synthesizing data

28.   Any four:
       a. accurate
       b. patient
       c. tenacious
       d. unprejudiced
       or moral
          honest
          imaginative
          versatile
          judgmental

29.   "And we know all things work together for good to them that love God, to them who are the called according to His purpose."

HISTORY & GEOGRAPHY 701

ALTERNATE LIFEPAC TEST

NAME _____

DATE _____

SCORE _____

95

119

Complete these sentences (each answer, 3 points).

1. History is the known story of man and his relationship toward a. _____ , b, _____ , and his c. _____ .

2. Three categories of history are a. _____ , b. _____ , and c. _____ .

3. Man's sinful nature is constant until he is _____ .

4. The three periods of history are _____ , _____ , and c. _____ .

5. Ephesians 6:10-19 tells us to put on the whole _____ of God.

6. Jesus met a woman at the well in _____ .

7. The two main sources a historian uses are a. _____ and b. _____ .

8. Two different types of evidence are a. _____ and b. _____ .

9. Two methods used to estimate the age of the earth are a. _____ and b. _____ .

Write the letter for the correct answer on each line (each answer, 2 points).

10. The idea of irrigation and embalming techniques was started by the _____ .
    a. Babylonians   b. Phoenicians   c. Egyptians   d. Hebrews

11. The alphabet and the spreading of civilized ideas in other lands were passed on to us by the
    _____ .
    a. Babylonians   b. Phoenicians   c. Egyptians   d. Hebrews

12. A system of weights and measures was introduced by the _____ .
    a. Babylonians   b. Phoenicians   c. Egyptians   d. Hebrews

13. The idea of one God and the Ten Commandments came from the _____ .
    a. Babylonians   b. Phoenicians   c. Egyptians   d. Hebrews

14. "There is no new thing under the sun" is found in _____ .
    a. Shakespeare   b. the Ten Commandments
    c. the Beatitudes   d. Ecclesiastes

15. The first civilization to develop a real sense of history was the _____ civilization.
    a. Babylonian   b. Phoenician   c. Egyptian   d. Hebrew

16. The problem with the Greek view of history is that it was _____ .
    a. inaccurate   b. incomplete   c. meaningless   d. sinful

17. Genesis, Exodus, Leviticus, Numbers, and Deuteronomy make up the _____ .
    a. Apocalypse   b. Gospels   c. Pentateuch   d. books of Poetry

18. Nebuchadnezzar's dream was interpreted by _____ .
    a. Moses   b. Joseph   c. David   d. Daniel

19. The view that history recurs purposelessly is called _____ .
    a. linear   b. cyclical   c. incomplete   d. inaccurate

Match these items (each answer, 2 points).

20. _____ epigrapher

21. _____ linguist

22. _____ numismatist

23. _____ statistician

24. _____ versatile

25. _____ tenacious

26. _____ speculate

a. one who can speak several languages

b. one skilled in collecting and arranging data

c. one who interprets ancient writings

d. to guess

e. one who studies history from remains of
   human culture

f. keeps on doing something until it is done

g. able to do many things well

h. one who studies coins, medals, or paper
   money

Complete these lists (each answer, 3 points).

27. List the five steps in the historical method.

a. _____   b. _____

c. _____   d. _____

e. _____

28. List four characteristics of a historian.

a. _____   b. _____

c. _____   d. _____

Complete this activity (this answer, 4 points).

29. Write Romans 8:28.

_____

_____

_____

_____

_____

HISTORY & GEOGRAPHY 702

Unit 2: What is Geography?

TEACHER NOTES

MATERIALS NEEDED FOR LIFEPAC	
Required	Suggested
None	• atlas • globe • encyclopedia or almanac • reference books or online sources

ADDITIONAL LEARNING ACTIVITIES

Section 1: Geography and the Planet Earth

1. Take a poll of students on where they are from or their ancestral heritage. As a class, compare the various climates represented.

2. Are any of the students planning to go into a field of science that was studied in this LIFEPAC? Which field?

3. Discuss what is being done to the mountains in some states (examples: houses built on mountainsides, highways built through them).

4. Would anyone in your class like to be an astronaut? Discuss qualifications needed.

5. Many people say there is not enough time to do the Lord's work. They say, "If I just had one extra day..." Point out that once every four years they do have an extra day. What will they do with it?

6. Discuss, what is the climate like where we live? Why do we have the climate that we do? For example, if you live at the seashore, your weather will be far different than if you live in the mountains. Have students explain the reasons for their climate.

7. Ask the following questions: When is your birthday? How is the earth tilted then? How does this tilt affect the weather at that time every year?

8. Ask the following questions: How would you determine how many times your parent's car or a neighbor's car may have been driven around the earth? If you know how many miles are on your parents' car, try to figure out how many times around the world it has traveled.

9. As a class, clip the daily weather forecast from the newspaper or printout from an online page each day for a week. Have students look back on the week to find out how accurate it was. Discuss, how do meteorologists predict the weather? Have a meteorologist speak to your class or locate interviews/video clips.

10. As a class, locate, in a magazine or on the internet, a satellite view of the earth. Find your city. Find other cities that members of the class come from. How did all of you actually travel over the face of the earth to get together in that one place?

11. Discuss the following with the class: When do the seasons begin and end every year? If you did not know these dates, how would you know the seasons had changed? Have students write a paragraph on each season.

12. Ask students, could you walk around the world, assuming you were strong enough, at the equator? Why or why not? Have students check a globe to be sure and explain their answer.

Section 2: Geography and Relief of the Earth

1. The LIFEPAC tells us that when flying in an airplane, hills and mountains rarely appear as high. Point out that, as Christians, we can live above the world, and the "mountains" in our lives do not appear to be so high. We can surmount them with God's help.

2. Ask students, do you think man should destroy mountains to build houses and highways?

3. Have students make a poster showing how a volcano works. Ask these questions: Where does its heat come from? Does its heat come to the surface of the earth in any other way? Is there any way man can make use of this energy?

4. Have students discuss in partners the various trips they have taken through this country. If anyone has been to a foreign country, have them share how the geography is different than it is here.

5. Assign students to research the geography of your state, and then write a report on the land features. They should be able to answer the following questions after research: What is the highest point? What is the lowest point?

6. Have the class gather samples of rocks in your area. See how many they can identify from their reference material. Ask the class, how old are they? Do they contain any fossils? Are any of them valuable to man?

Section 3: Maps and the Study of Our World

1. Have students use a map of the world or the United States in order to describe and discuss the various time zones.

2. Discuss the "jet lag" some people get from traveling on airplanes. Why does this happen?

3. Find as many different types of maps as possible and explain them to the class. Discuss the following questions: Why are there so many different kinds? What does each type do?

4. Choose three cities, including your own. Have students use a globe to locate them, as close as possible, by their latitude and longitude.

5. Have the class use a common road map to make a chart showing all the symbols used on the map and what they mean.

6. How does a compass work? What are the principles involved? Try to locate a compass and see if you can make it work for you.

Administer the LIFEPAC Test

The test is to be administered in one session. Give no help except with directions.
Evaluate the tests and review areas where the students have done poorly.
Review the pages and activities that stress the concepts tested.
If necessary, administer the Alternate LIFEPAC Test.

ANSWER KEYS

SECTION 1

1.1 ACROSS   DOWN
    1. savanna   1. steppe
    2. elevation   2. taiga
    3. rainforest   3. topography
    4. tropical jungle   4. tundra

1.2 a. physical
    b. people

1.3 a. land
    b. stream

1.4 a. plain
    b. plateau
    c. mountain

1.5 a. ionosphere
    b. stratosphere
    c. troposphere

1.6 Any order:
    a. condensation
    b. air masses
    c. wind systems
    d. cyclones
    e. temperature
    f. forecasting
    g. precipitation
    h. evaporation
    i. fronts

1.7 b
1.8 d
1.9 f
1.10 g
1.11 e
1.12 c
1.13 a
1.14 atmosphere
1.15 climatology
1.16 Climate
1.17 Any order:
    a. temperature
    b. pressure
    c. wind
    d. moisture

1.18 Any order:
    a. wind belts
    b. altitude
    c. pressure belts
    d. ocean currents
    e. relationships between continents and oceans
    f. topography

1.19 commercial activities
1.20 governments
1.21 city growth
1.22 mathematical
1.23 imperfect sphere
1.24 c
1.25 a
1.26 b
1.27 e
1.28 The study of a society's activities, beliefs, institutions, and behavior patterns.
1.29 The method of studying an area by applying the principles of all branches of geography to a given area.
1.30 a. Mariana Trench
    b. 36,198
1.31 a. Mt. Everest
    b. 29,028
1.32 12
1.33 a. mountains
    b. hills
    c. plateaus
    d. plains
1.34 f
1.35 a
1.36 b
1.37 e
1.38 d
1.39 a. 24
    b. axis
1.40 a. six
    b. six
1.41 c
1.42 h
1.43 d
1.44 j
1.45 a
1.46 f
1.47 g
1.48 e
1.49 i
1.50 b
1.51 Teacher check

SELF TEST 1

1.01 b
1.02 d
1.03 a
1.04 d
1.05 c
1.06 b
1.07 a
1.08 b
1.09 d
1.010 a
1.011 c
1.012 Any order:
    a. ionosphere
    b. stratosphere
    c. troposphere
1.013 Any order:
    a. temperature
    b. pressure
    c. moisture
    d. wind
1.014 a. Mt. Everest
    b. Mariana Trench
1.015 meteorology
1.016 Cultural
1.017 Urban
1.018 a. land
    b. stream
1.019 climate
1.020 a. Arctic
    b. Antarctic
1.021 f
1.022 c
1.023 d
1.024 b
1.025 a
1.026 e
1.027 The tilt of the earth points the poles away from the sun in alternate seasons. The sun never rises in the winter at the North Pole nor does it set in the summer. The opposite is true at the South Pole.
1.028 The earth is an imperfect sphere. It is slightly flattened at the poles and bulges at the equator.

SECTION 2

2.1 c
2.2 e
2.3 g
2.4 i
2.5 a
2.6 j
2.7 h
2.8 f
2.9 d
2.10 b
2.11 a. flat
    b. sea
2.12 silt
2.13 "Gift of the Nile"
2.14 lowlands
2.15 a. trade
    b. manufacturing
2.16 a. 1,000 miles
    b. Amazon
2.17 rainfall
2.18 alluvial
2.19 Either order:
    a. Flood waters spread sand and gravel on the plains instead of rich soil.
    b. The water on the land cannot drain, leaving it damp and hard to cultivate.
2.20 Any order:
    a. North American Plains
    b. Eurasian Plains
    c. Amazon Basin
2.21 The area the North American Plains covers is from the Rockies to the Appalachian Mountains and from the Gulf of Mexico to the Arctic Ocean.
2.22 Either order:
    a. Europe
    b. Asia
2.23 a. hill
    b. water
    or rain
2.24 a. Roads and railroads must wind up steep slopes.
    b. Bridges must be built to level the route.
2.25 Mt. Everest
2.26 vertical
2.27 one degree
2.28 Any order:
    a. barriers *or* boundaries
    b. mining for minerals
    c. grazing
    d. lumbering
    e. recreation

2.29 a. folding
b. faulting

2.30 They prevent moisture-laden winds from reaching dry areas.

2.31 Moisture-laden winds that blow against high mountains are forced up into the cooler altitudes. The sudden drop in temperature causes the water vapor to condense and come down in the form of rain.

2.32 a

2.33 b

2.34 a

2.35 a

2.36 c

2.37 b

2.38 c

2.39 a

2.40 b

2.41 a

2.42 d

2.43 c

2.44 true

2.45 true

2.46 false

2.47 true

2.48 false

2.49 true

2.50 a

2.51 b

2.52 b

2.53 a

2.54 c

2.55 c

2.56 seventy percent

2.57 Any order:
a. Atlantic
b. Pacific
c. Indian
d. Arctic

2.58 land

2.59 continental shelf

2.60 Either order
a. oil
b. coal

2.61 Either order:
a. Labrador Current
b. Gulf Stream
or North Atlantic Drift

2.62 Because the water never gets too cold in the winter or too hot in the summer, the ocean temperature remains somewhat uniform. The winds blowing in from the ocean raise the temperature in winter and help keep the temperature cooler in the summer. The continuous movement of the ocean currents have the greatest effect on climate. The warm water from the Gulf Stream, for example, helps keep the colder waters of the North Atlantic ice-free in the winter for the British Isles, and the winds blowing in from this current warm the land. The cold Labrador Current has just the opposite effect on the northern United States.

2.63 3,000

2.64 a. agriculture
b. manufacturing

2.65 3,000 feet

2.66 a. east
b. west

2.67 a. Central
b. Great

2.68 conifers

2.69 Great Basin

2.70 a. Sierra Nevada
b. Coast

2.71 Teacher check

2.72 Teacher check

2.73 Teacher check

SELF TEST 2

2.01 a. Amazon
     b. North American
     c. Eurasian
2.02 a. Atlantic
     b. Pacific
     c. Indian
     d. Arctic
2.03 a. Central Lowlands
     b. Great Plains
2.04 estuary
2.05 b
2.06 c
2.07 a
2.08 c
2.09 d
2.010 i
2.011 g
2.012 k
2.013 a
2.014 c
2.015 j
2.016 h
2.017 f
2.018 b
2.019 a
2.020 b
2.021 d
2.022 c
2.023 Any order:
     a. mountains
     b. hills
     c. plains
     d. plateaus
2.024 a
2.025 a
2.026 b
2.027 c
2.028 b
2.029 c
2.030 a
2.031 b
2.032 c
2.033 c
2.034 a

SECTION 3

3.1 ACROSS
     1. longitude
     2. contour line
     3. hachure marks
     4. projection
     DOWN
     1. latitude
     2. isotherm
3.2 f
3.3 c
3.4 d
3.5 a
3.6 b
3.7 true
3.8 true
3.9 true
3.10 false
3.11 false
3.12 true
3.13 true
3.14 a. North Pole
     b. South Pole
3.15 360
3.16 prime meridian
3.17 longitude
3.18 a. Western hemisphere
     b. Eastern hemisphere
3.19 west longitude
3.20 B
3.21 A
3.22 F
3.23 G
3.24 E
3.25 H
3.26 C
3.27 120
3.28 130
3.29 30
3.30 B
3.31 A
3.32 M
3.33 G
3.34 J
3.35 E
3.36 L
3.37 50
3.38 110
3.39 90
3.40 equator
3.41 a. Southern hemisphere
     b. Northern hemisphere

3.42	zero degrees
3.43	90 degrees
3.44	e
3.45	c
3.46	a
3.47	f
3.48	b
3.49	Teacher check
3.50	a. Eastern
	b. Central
	c. Mountain
	d. Pacific
3.51	15 degrees
3.52	a. 24
	b. 15
3.53	time zones
3.54	lose
3.55	180 degrees

SELF TEST 3

3.01	c
3.02	b
3.03	d
3.04	a
3.05	c
3.06	a
3.07	c
3.08	c
3.09	d
3.010	a
3.011	h
3.012	c
3.013	k
3.014	g
3.015	f
3.016	i
3.017	a
3.018	d
3.019	e
3.020	b
3.021	Any three:
	a. Rocky
	b. Appalachian
	c. Cascade
	or Sierra Nevada
3.022	Any order:
	a. interrupted-area
	b. Mercator
	c. polar
3.023	Either oder:
	a. Northern hemisphere
	b. Southern hemisphere
3.024	Either order:
	a. Eastern hemisphere
	b. Western hemisphere
3.025	Any order:
	a. Eastern
	b. Mountain
	c. Central
	d. Pacific
3.026	globe
3.027	typographical
3.028	political
3.029	climate
3.030	population
3.031	road

LIFEPAC TEST

1. true
2. false
3. false
4. true
5. true
6. true
7. true
8. false
9. false
10. true
11. true
12. true
13. false
14. true
15. true
16. Any order:
    a. mountains
    b. hills
    c. plains
    d. plateaus
17. a. Rocky
    b. Appalachian
    c. Cascade
    or Sierra Nevada
18. cultural geography
19. climatology
20. Mariana Trench
21. b
22. b
23. a
24. a, b, *or* d
25. a
26. d
27. b
28. a
29. d
30. b

31.-40.

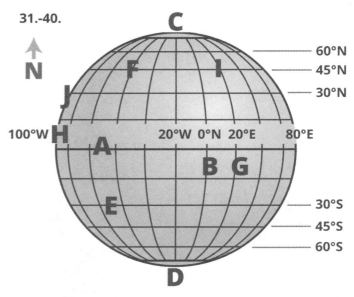

41. Geography is the study of the earth's surface, climate, continents, countries, peoples, industries, and products as they relate to people.

ALTERNATE LIFEPAC TEST

1. h
2. e
3. n
4. a
5. l
6. p
7. s
8. r
9. j
10. d
11. b
12. f
13. u
14. o
15. t
16. g
17. k
18. c
19. m
20. i
21. Any two:
   a. physical
   b. meteorology
   or climatology
      economic
      urban
      political,
      mathematical
      cultural
      regional
22. Any order:
   a. land erosion
   b. weathering
   c. stream erosion
   or formation and effect of plains, plateaus,
      mountains, and rivers; work of ice, ocean,
      shorelines, and atmosphere; plant and
      animal distribution
23. Any two:
   a. troposphere
   b. stratosphere
   or ionosphere
24. Any two:
   a. rainforests
   b. tropical jungles
   or savannas, steppes, deserts, taigas, tundras
25. Either order:
   a. North Pole
   b. South Pole
26. a. June 21
   b. December 21

27. Any two:
   a. North American Plains
   b. Eurasian Plains
   or Amazon Basin
28. Either order:
   a. Mercator
   b. polar projection
   or interrupted-area projection
29. Either order:
   a. political
   b. physical
   or population
      land use
      climatic
      road

30.-39.

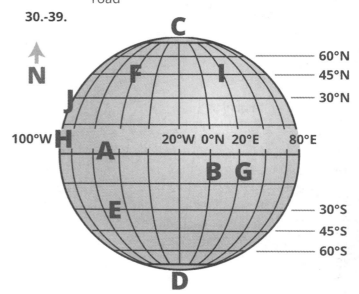

40. At the North Pole, the sun never completely
   sets in the summer and in the winter it never
   rises over the horizon. The reverse is true of
   the South Pole.

HISTORY & GEOGRAPHY 702

ALTERNATE LIFEPAC TEST

NAME _____

DATE _____

SCORE _____

98 / 122

Match these items (each answer, 2 points).

1. _____ elevation
2. _____ savanna
3. _____ taiga
4. _____ geography
5. _____ climatology
6. _____ Mt. Everest
7. _____ 365¼ days
8. _____ solstice
9. _____ Tropic of Cancer
10. _____ alluvial
11. _____ Egypt
12. _____ Amazon Basin
13. _____ March 21
14. _____ water
15. _____ December 21
16. _____ tributary
17. _____ polar projection
18. _____ equator
19. _____ International Date Line
20. _____ 24,860 miles

a. earth description
b. Gift of the Nile
c. represents 0°
d. formed by sediment
e. grassy plain with few or no trees
f. third major plain area
g. branch of a river
h. height above sea level
i. circumference from pole to pole
j. imaginary line
k. air-age map
l. study of climate
m. 180° longitude
n. a swampy forest
o. 70 percent of the globe
p. highest point above sea level
q. distance from sun
r. equal day
s. complete trip around the sun
t. shortest day of the year
u. spring equinox

Complete these sentences (each answer, 3 points).

21. Two different classes of geography are a. _____ and

    b. _____ .

22. Three changes that occur on the earth's surface are a. _____ ,

    b. _____ , and c. _____ .

23. Meteorology deals with three parts of the atmosphere. Two of these parts are

    a. _____ and b. _____ .

24. Two types of climatic regions are a. _____ and

    b. _____ .

25. During each twenty-four hour rotation of the earth, most places on earth—except two—
    experience a period of light and a period of darkness. The two exceptions are the

    a. _____ and the b. _____ .

26. The longest day of the year is a. _____ and the shortest day is

    b. _____ .

27. Two of the plains regions are a. _____ and

    b. _____ .

28. Two different types of map projections are a. _____ and

    b. _____ .

29. Two different kinds of maps are a. _____ and

    b. _____ .

Place the letter for each of the following locations on the map (each answer, 2 points).

30. B on the prime meridian

31. A on the equator

32. C on the North Pole

33. D on the South Pole

34. G on 20 degrees east longitude

35. F on 45 degrees north latitude

36. E on 30 degrees south latitude

37. H on 100 degrees west longitude

38. J on 30 degrees north latitude and 100 degrees west longitude

39. I on 45 degrees north latitude and 20 degrees east longitude

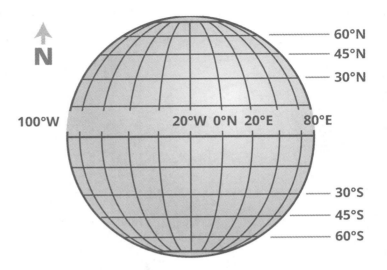

Answer the following question (this answer, 5 points).

40. Why do the polar regions have six months of light and six months of darkness?

_____

_____

_____

_____

_____

HISTORY & GEOGRAPHY 703

Unit 3: U.S. History and Geography

TEACHER NOTES

MATERIALS NEEDED FOR LIFEPAC	
Required	Suggested
None	• map of the United States • atlas • encyclopedia • almanac • reference books or online sources

ADDITIONAL LEARNING ACTIVITIES

Section 1: Looking at the United States

1. Using a physical-political wall map, review with the class how mountain ranges, wide dry plains, rivers, and swamp lands affected patterns of settlement in the United States. Include a discussion of early transportation and communication.

2. On a geographical-terms chart, review the meaning of common geographical terms such as *plateau*, *delta*, and *river basin*. See how much students remember from History & Geography LIFEPAC 702.

3. As a class, make a wall map to show the various routes followed by early explorers of North America.

4. Americans have always loved the beautiful physical country in which they live. As a class, collect and share songs and poems that express this love of the land, particular rivers, mountains, plains, and so forth (example: "Home On the Range").

5. Obtain a detailed map of your own country. Have students locate rivers, deltas, mountains, bays, peninsulas, and other geographical features.

6. Have students research the Viking explorers and report to class.

7. Assign a report on one of the early settlements, such as Jamestown, Quebec, or St. Augustine.

Section 2: Physical and Cultural Regions of the Northeast and the South

1. Review with the class three measures of climate, how they are measured, and how they are reported: annual rainfall, mean temperature, elevation, and humidity.

2. Discuss the factors that promote agricultural development and those that favor manufacturing. Use local examples where possible.

3. Have small groups compare population, annual rainfall, mean temperatures, important products, and scenic attractions of five states in your region.

4. Hold a mock debate on slavery in which some students represent slaveholders and some abolitionists, who wished to end slavery. Make sure that you have mature students for this activity, and explain that students are representing historical perspectives.

5. Introduce the following scenario for an activity: Imagine that your family is going to move to one of the cities of a region you have never visited. Find out information that will help you in preparing for the change and adjusting to your new home.

6. Have students make a report on Eli Whitney's other important invention, the cotton gin, and its effect on the South.

7. Have students use state maps to find five to ten interesting place names in the Northeast and South, and do research to find out the origin of the names.

Section 3: Physical and Cultural Regions of the Midwest and the West

1. Discuss the forces that affected the settlement of the Midwest and West. Include the Homestead Act, irrigation projects, development of railroads, the California Gold Rush, and the Civil War.

2. Using a map, review the important national parks and discuss the significance of the national park system.

3. Have different class members find out about the population per square mile in several Western states, and compare this to several Eastern states. What are the reasons for these differences? What effect do they have on daily life, ways of making a living, and government?

4. For the duration of the work on this LIFEPAC, make your classroom a "gallery of America" by putting up colored pictures that show the variety of landscapes and ways of life in this country.

5. Discuss the popular ideas about cowboys and life in Hawaii and Alaska. To what extent are these pictures true?

6. Assign students to report on one historic event that effected the development of the region west of the Mississippi, such as the Gold Rush, the purchase of Alaska, or the boundary dispute between British and Americans over the Oregon Territory.

Administer the LIFEPAC Test

The test is to be administered in one session. Give no help except with directions.
Evaluate the tests and review areas where the students have done poorly.
Review the pages and activities that stress the concepts tested.
If necessary, administer the Alternate LIFEPAC Test.

» ADDITIONAL ACTIVITY

The answer key on the following page applies to the additional activity.

» ADDITIONAL ACTIVITY ANSWER KEY

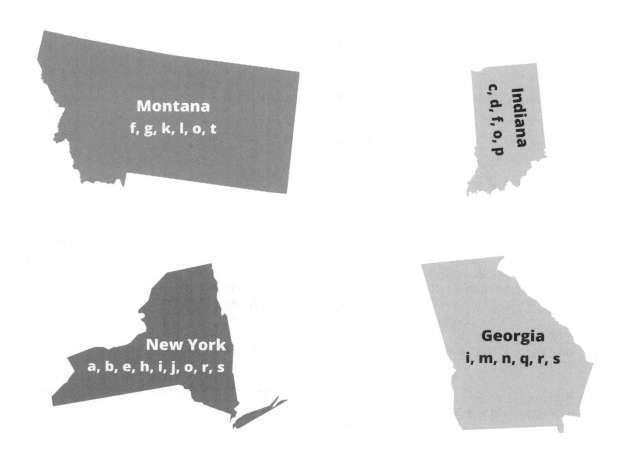

Montana
f, g, k, l, o, t

Indiana
c, d, f, o, p

New York
a, b, e, h, i, j, o, r, s

Georgia
i, m, n, q, r, s

The additional activity on the following page may be reproduced as a student worksheet.

» ADDITIONAL ACTIVITY

Which State is it?

Here are the outline maps of four states typical of the various regions. First identity each state by name. Then look at the list of natural resources, crops, physical features, and events. Put the letter which identifies each one into the proper state outline. If an item can be found in more than one state, enter it in all that apply. Use common sense.

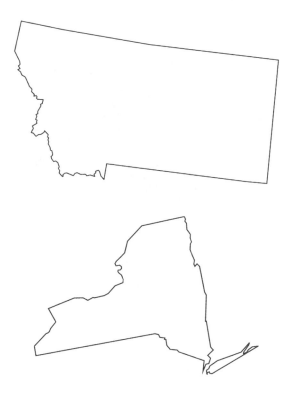

a. settled by the Dutch
b. large cities; dense population
c. Midwestern
d. cattle and dairy
e. Catskill Mountains
f. copper mines
g. dry farming methods
h. Hudson River
i. fishing
j. Industrial Revolution began

k. Intermountain Region
l. Rocky Mountains
m. mild winters
n. cotton fields
o. long, cold winters
p. corn fields
q. Southern state
r. port cities
s. one of thirteen original colonies
t. limited rainfall

ANSWER KEYS

SECTION 1

1.1 b
1.2 d
1.3 f
1.4 h
1.5 g
1.6 e
1.7 c
1.8 a
1.9 ACROSS
1. political region
2. natural region
3. plateau
4. landform
5. elevation
DOWN
1. peninsula
2. gorge
3. glacier
1.10 Any two:
a. Africa
b. South America
or Asia
1.11 Capricorn
1.12 Cancer
1.13 12:30 P.M.
1.14 6:00 A.M.
1.15 a. ocean
b. sea
1.16 Any order:
a. U.S.A.
b. Canada
c. Caribbean Islands
d. Greenland
e. Mexico
f. Central America
1.17 Alaska
1.18 Hawaii
1.19 Appalachian
1.20 Any order:
a. Blue Ridge
b. Adirondack
c. Black
d. Catskill
e. Great Smokey
f. White
g. Green
or Allegheny
1.21 Piedmont

1.22 a. Pacific Coast
b. Intermountain
c. Rocky
1.23 a. Atlantic
b. Gulf
c. Central
d. Great
e. Superior
f. Ozark
g. Appalachian
1.24 Any order:
a. Mississippi
b. Missouri
c. Tennessee
d. Ohio
1.25 a. Appalachian
b. Great
1.26 a
1.27 c
1.28 b
1.29 a
1.30 b
1.31 a
1.32 b
1.33 c
1.34 Any order:
a. Sierra Nevada
b. Cascade
c. Coast Range
1.35 c
1.36 e
1.37 a
1.38 d
1.39 b
1.40 true
1.41 false
1.42 true
1.43 true
1.44 c
1.45 b
1.46 b
1.47 c
1.48 b
1.49 b
1.50 a

1.51	Connecticut
	Delaware
	Georgia
	Maryland
	Massachusetts
	New Hampshire
	New Jersey
	New York
	North Carolina
	Pennsylvania
	Rhode Island
	South Carolina
	Virginia
1.52	fifteen
1.53	Any order:
	a. Kentucky
	b. Tennessee
	c. Vermont
1.54	Any order:
	a. Arizona
	b. Alaska
	c. New Mexico
	d. Hawaii
	e. Oklahoma

SELF TEST 1

1.01	c
1.02	e
1.03	d
1.04	h
1.05	g
1.06	b
1.07	a
1.08	f
1.09	i
1.010	j
1.011	true
1.012	false
1.013	false
1.014	true
1.015	false
1.016	false
1.017	true
1.018	true
1.019	false
1.020	true
1.021	b
1.022	b
1.023	a
1.024	c
1.025	b
1.026	b
1.027	Any order:
	a. Europe
	b. Asia
	c. Africa
	d. Antarctica
	e. Australia
	f. North America
	g. South America

SECTION 2

2.1	c	**2.21**	true
2.2	e	**2.22**	true
2.3	g	**2.23**	false
2.4	a	**2.24**	true
2.5	f	**2.25**	false
2.6	d	**2.26**	false
2.7	b	**2.27**	a. Pilgrims *or* Separatists

2.8 New York

2.9 Rhode Island

2.10 Maryland

2.11 Any order:
  a. Maryland
  b. Delaware
  c. New Jersey
  d. New York
  e. Connecticut
  f. Rhode Island
  g. Massachusetts
  h. Maine
  i. New Hampshire

2.12 Any order:
  a. Maine
  b. New Hampshire
  c. Vermont
  d. New York

2.13 Any three:
  a. Green
  b. White
  c. Adirondack
  or Allegheny
    Catskill

2.14 Any order:
  a. Chesapeake
  b. Delaware
  c. New York

2.15 Either order:
  a. Ontario
  b. Erie

2.16 a. ice glaciers
  b. holes

2.17 a. equator
  b. water
  c. altitude

2.18 Niagara

2.19 Champlain

2.20 Any order:
  a. Connecticut
  b. Hudson
  c. Pawcatuck
  d. Susquehanna
  e. Mohawk

2.27 b. Puritans

2.28 Puritans

2.29 Revolutionary

2.30 d

2.31 a

2.32 c

2.33 Any order:
  a. Florida
  b. Georgia
  c. South Carolina
  d. North Carolina
  e. Virginia

2.34 Any order:
  a. Florida
  b. Alabama
  c. Mississippi
  d. Louisiana

2.35 a. lowland

2.36 Any five in any order:
  a. Macon, Georgia
  b. Richmond, Virginia
  c. Baltimore, Maryland
  d. Raleigh, North Carolina
  e. Columbia, South Carolina
  or Columbus, GA, Augusta, GA,
    Washington DC, Philadelphia, PA

2.37 It is a wide, flat area.
  It has a rocky surface.
  Waterfalls form at the downriver edge.

2.38 Any four:
  a. Ohio
  b. Mississippi
  c. Alabama
  d. Tennessee
  or Savannah, Shenandoah

2.39 a. Gulf
  b. Atlantic

2.40 June

2.41 August

2.42 b. humid

2.43 b. rented

2.44 c. Appomattox Courthouse

2.45 b. John Wilkes Booth

2.46 a. 1861-1865

SELF TEST 2

2.01	c
2.02	f
2.03	e
2.04	i
2.05	b
2.06	a
2.07	j
2.08	d
2.09	g
2.010	k
2.011	false
2.012	true
2.013	true
2.014	false
2.015	true
2.016	true
2.017	true
2.018	false
2.019	true
2.020	false
2.021	c. political
2.022	a. Vermont
2.023	a. oldest
2.024	c. coastal plains
2.025	c. waterfalls
2.026	Pilgrims *or* Separatists
2.027	Any order:
	a. France
	b. Spain
	c. England
2.028	Either order:
	a. Atlantic
	b. Pacific
2.029	1959
2.030	a. equator
	b. water
	c. altitude
2.031	Waterfalls
2.032	Reconstruction
2.033	Northeast
2.034	tenant farming

SECTION 3

3.1	Michigan
3.2	Lake Superior
3.3	Lake Michigan
3.4	Any order:
	Ohio, Michigan, Indiana,
	Wisconsin, Illinois, Minnesota
3.5	ACROSS
	1. blizzard
	2. mission
	3. tornado
	DOWN
	1. levee
	2. rain shadow
3.6	Either order:
	a. elevation
	b. rainfall
3.7	b. continental
3.8	a. rain shadow
	b. Rocky
3.9	Canada
3.10	Any three:
	a. Ohio
	b. Missouri
	c. Mississippi
	or Rio Grande
3.11	Erosion
3.12	tornadoes
3.13	c
3.14	f
3.15	g
3.16	e
3.17	a
3.18	b
3.19	d
3.20	a, d
3.21	Any order:
	a. corn belt
	b. wheat belt
	c. hay and dairy belts
3.22	fertile
3.23	grazing
3.24	Chisholm
3.25	Either order:
	a. Lewis
	b. Clark
3.26	Oklahoma
3.27	Cumberland
3.28	Cyrus McCormick
3.29	Texas, New Mexico, Arizona, California

3.30 Any order:
   a. Arizona
   b. Utah
   c. New Mexico
   d. Colorado
3.31 Any order:
   a. Alaska
   b. Washington
   c. Idaho
   d. Montana
3.32 Grand Canyon
3.33 Any order:
   a. Cascades
   b. Sierra Nevada
   c. Coast Ranges
3.34 Whitney
3.35 Great Basin
3.36 Any four:
   a. Columbia
   b. Snake
   c. Willamette
   d. Sacramento
   or Yukon
      Colorado
3.37 February
3.38 July
3.39 Any three:
   a. iron
   b. copper
   c. gold
   or zinc
      silver
      lead
      tungsten
      uranium
3.40 redwood
3.41 apples
3.42 Any order:
   a. pineapple
   b. sugar cane
   c. coffee
3.43 Nuestra Senora la Reina de los Angeles
   or Los Angeles
3.44 Spanish
3.45 missions
3.46 cattle
3.47 Sir Francis Drake
3.48 gold
3.49 Great Britain
   or England
3.50 Homestead

SELF TEST 3

3.01 false
3.02 true
3.03 false
3.04 false
3.05 true
3.06 false
3.07 false
3.08 true
3.09 false
3.010 false
3.011 b
3.012 c
3.013 b
3.014 a
3.015 b
3.016 c
3.017 a
3.018 b
3.019 b
3.020 c
3.021 Spanish
3.022 Homestead
3.023 waterfalls
3.024 Oklahoma
3.025 Either order:
   a. Atlantic
   b. Pacific
3.026 b
3.027 d
3.028 f
3.029 h
3.030 i
3.031 g
3.032 e
3.033 c
3.034 a

LIFEPAC TEST

1. c
2. a
3. b
4. a
5. b
6. d
7. c
8. a
9. d
10. b
11. a
12. c
13. c
14. c
15. c
16. a
17. d
18. b
19. c
20. d
21. c. the Appalachians
22. c. coastal plains
23. b. Michigan
24. a. Midwest
25. c. 1787
26. b. Holland
27. a. Jefferson Davis
28. c. Appalachian Highlands
29. a. Spain
30. c. Hawaii
31. false
32. true
33. false
34. false
35. true
36. false
37. true
38. false
39. true
40. false
41.-44. Teacher check

ALTERNATE LIFEPAC TEST

1. a
2. d
3. b
4. b
5. d
6. a
7. c
8. d
9. c
10. b
11. c
12. a
13. c
14. d
15. d
16. a
17. b
18. d
19. a
20. c
21. Teacher check
22. Teacher check
23. Teacher check
24. b. a method of making gun parts which were interchangeable
25. true
26. false
27. true
28. true
29. false
30. false
31. false
32. contiguous
33. delta
34. Sierra Nevada
    or Cascade; Coast Range
35. plateau *or* mesa
36. Atlantic
37. rain shadow
38. Lake Michigan
39. glaciers
40. fall line
41. mild *or* warm

HISTORY & GEOGRAPHY 703

ALTERNATE LIFEPAC TEST

NAME _____

DATE _____

SCORE _____

Write the letter in the blank that tells where the following products, historical events, natural features, or climatic conditions belong (each answer, 2 points).

1. _____ Plymouth Colony
2. _____ lumbering; fishing; mining
3. _____ the Everglades
4. _____ rice; cotton; peanuts
5. _____ large areas of dry soil
6. _____ explored by Henry Hudson
7. _____ breadbasket of America
8. _____ Rocky Mountains
9. _____ Badlands and Black Hills
10. _____ Civil War battlefields
11. _____ Louisiana Purchase
12. _____ battlefields of American Revolution
13. _____ Mississippi River Basin
14. _____ an island state
15. _____ explored by Coronado
16. _____ many of largest cities
17. _____ sugar plantations
18. _____ Colorado River
19. _____ large factories
20. _____ corn; pork; wheat

a. Northeast region
b. Southern region
c. Midwest region
d. Western region

Write the letter for the correct answer on each line (each answer, 2 points).

21. My own state is in the _____ region of the United States.
    a. Northeastern   b. Southern   c. Midwestern   d. Western

22. The largest city in my own state is on _____ .
    a. a salt water harbor
    b. a Great Lakes harbor
    c. a large river
    d. none of these

23. I live _____ .
    a. east of the Appalachian Highlands
    b. in the Central Lowlands
    c. west of the Continental Divide
    d. in one of the two states which have no contiguous states
    e. on the eastern slopes of the Rocky Mountains

24. Eli Whitney invented _____ .
    a. the automobile
    b. a method of making gun parts which were interchangeable
    c. a steam engine for Mississippi riverboats
    d. a mechanical reaping machine

Answer *true* **or** *false* (each answer, 1 point).

25. _____ The Hawaiian Islands were formed by volcanic action.

26. _____ The Homestead Act kept settlers from traveling west.

27. _____ The Southern states have many navigable rivers.

28. _____ The Rio Grande is on the border between Texas and Mexico.

29. _____ The growing season is the period of time between harvest and planting, usually autumn to spring.

30. _____ Vikings from Norway first explored the Pacific Coast.

31. _____ The fiftieth state was admitted to the Union in 1898.

Complete these statements (each answer, 3 points).

32. Neighboring states with common borders are said to be _____ .

33. Land deposited by a river at its mouth is called a(n) _____ .

34. One mountain range which runs parallel to the Pacific Coast is _____

    _____ .

35. A high, flat piece of land is called a(n) _____ .

36. The Appalachian Mountains run parallel to the _____ Ocean.

37. Land on the inland side of a mountain range that receives little moisture is said to be in the

    _____ .

38. The Great Lake that lies entirely within United States borders is _____

    _____ .

39. Land in the New England states is rocky and thin because much of its topsoil was scoured off

    by _____ .

40. Cities east of the Appalachians which were established at the sites of waterfalls are called

    _____ cities.

41. The winters in the Southern region are usually _____ .

HISTORY & GEOGRAPHY 704

Unit 4: Anthropology

TEACHER NOTES

MATERIALS NEEDED FOR LIFEPAC	
Required	Suggested
None	• atlas • encyclopedia • reference books or online sources

ADDITIONAL LEARNING ACTIVITIES

Section 1: The Study of Man

1. Discuss the differences between anthropologists and other scientists, such as astronomers biologists, physicists, and so forth. What do anthropologists do that no other scientists do?

2. Have students keep a diary of a week in their school life as if they were field workers from another society. Have them read portions of their diaries aloud.

3. Have partners discuss a foreign society that they find interesting. After students have explained their reasoning and impressions to a partner, tell students to think about bias that may have been presented in this discussion. The purpose of this activity is for students to consider how they may have shown bias or prejudice.

4. Have students discuss the major features of American culture today: Of what features do you think God approves? Of what features do you think God disapproves?

5. Obtain a new or used copy of *National Geographic* magazine. Have students find a story about a culture that is completely different from their own. Discuss as a class: What methods do you think the author used to learn what they did? Would you enjoy being a member of that culture?

6. Ask students, if an archaeologist a thousand years from now goes through the remains of your house, what will they find? What will it tell them about you? If you left a note behind for them to read so they could understand you better, what would the note say?

7. Assign students to write a 250-word report on the discovery of the tomb of King Tutankhamen by an archaeologist.

Section 2: The Nature of Man

1. Discuss ways in which all people everywhere are the same. Are people all alike physically? Do all people have a religion? A language? A government?

2. Discuss the following with the class: How does the Bible tell us the different races were formed? How and why do ethnic groups change over time?

3. Have partners discuss how people around the world are different from one another: Does this difference lead to wars? If not, what does?

4. Assign students to write a short paper describing how they would interact and learn from an acquaintance from another country. Provide this scenario: Your new acquaintance is totally different in appearance from you, they dress differently from anyone you have ever seen, and they do not speak any English. This person wants to be friends. What would you do? How would you communicate and learn about one another?

5. As a class, make a bulletin board of pictures and facts illustrating the similarities and differences between peoples.

Section 3: The Culture of Man

1. If possible, invite an anthropologist or a missionary to visit the class.

2. Discuss these questions with the class: How has man affected his environment? Has the effect been all good, all bad, or some of each?

3. Set up this activity: What is a potlatch? Hold an imaginary potlatch among your friends, giving away your valuable possessions one by one until they are gone. Do you see any reason for such a ceremony? Why, or why not?

4. Have students plan some meals they would have if they lived in a strictly horticultural society. Students can exchange meal plans. Discuss, would you enjoy this kind of diet?

5. Have students read the entry about "anthropology" in an encyclopedia or online and write a brief summary of it.

6. Discuss how the "rites of passage" are conducted in the United States.

Administer the LIFEPAC Test

The test is to be administered in one session. Give no help except with directions.
Evaluate the tests and review areas where the students have done poorly.
Review the pages and activities that stress the concepts tested.
If necessary, administer the Alternate LIFEPAC Test.

ANSWER KEYS

SECTION 1

1.1 ACROSS
1. generalization
2. haphazard
3. contemporary
4. comprehensive
5. band
6. ethnographer

DOWN
1. genealogical
2. ethics
3. etiquette
4. bias
5. divination
6. folklore

1.2 "the science of humanity"
1.3 ethnologists
1.4 past
1.5 physical anthropologists
1.6 archaeologists
1.7 c
1.8 e
1.9 g
1.10 i
1.11 k
1.12 a
1.13 j
1.14 h
1.15 f
1.16 d
1.17 b
1.18 Either order:
a. ancient
b. modern
1.19 The nonliterate peoples were dying out.
Passing ways of life need to be recorded.
1.20 c
1.21 b
1.22 d
1.23 d
1.24 The goal of anthropology is to discover
the similarities in human custom between
groups.
1.25 He discovered that birth, puberty, marriage,
and death are always accompanied by
ceremonies.

1.26 a. birth
1.27 b. puberty
1.28 c. marriage
1.29 d. death
1.30 a. birth
1.31 b. puberty
1.32 d. death
1.33 c. marriage
1.34 Any order:
a. trade
b. games
c. toolmaking
d. personal names
e. music
1.35 The cooperative method in anthropology
compares similarities and differences
among societies.
1.36 a. regularities
b. world-wide
c. culture
1.37 The following items should be checked:
✓ evaluate culture from native person's
point of view
✓ live among the people and participate
in their culture
1.38 d
1.39 f
1.40 g
1.41 a
1.42 e
1.43 b
1.44 false
1.45 true
1.46 false
1.47 false
1.48 true
1.49 participant observation
1.50 key informants
1.51 a. psychological
b. life
1.52 genealogical
1.53 census

1.54	b
1.55	c
1.56	a
1.57	c
1.58	a
1.59	d
1.60	a
1.61	c
1.62	b
1.63	c
1.64	b

SELF TEST 1

1.01	c	
1.02	e	
1.03	g	
1.04	i	
1.05	k	
1.06	m	
1.07	a	
1.08	o	
1.09	n	
1.010	l	
1.011	j	
1.012	h	
1.013	f	
1.014	d	
1.015	b	
1.016	b.	universals
1.017	d.	holistic
1.018	c.	regularities
1.019	a.	culture
1.020	b.	all seasonal activities
1.021	b.	God
1.022	d.	holistic
1.023	a.	they are dying out
1.024	4	
1.025	3	
1.026	8	
1.027	6	
1.028	1	
1.029	5	
1.030	10	
1.031	7	
1.032	2	
1.033	9	
1.034	language	
1.035	comparative	
1.036	ethnocentrism	

1.037 Either order:
a. kinship chart
b. census

1.038 culture shock

1.039 participant

1.040 The following items should be checked:
✓ greetings
✓ feasting
✓ law
✓ family
✓ property rights
✓ ethics

SECTION 2

2.1   f
2.2   d
2.3   b
2.4   a
2.5   c
2.6   e
2.7   g
2.8   Eve
2.9   a. God
         b. created
         c. image
2.10 dust
2.11 206
2.12 man (Adam)
2.13 ACROSS
         1. heterozygous
         2. allele
         3. gene pool
         DOWN
         1. homozygous
         2. taxa
         3. genus
2.14 God
2.15 rule
2.16 shadow
2.17 a. conscious
         b. responsibility
2.18 true
2.19 false
2.20 true
2.21 true
2.22 Either order:
         a. sin
         b. death
2.23 everlasting
2.24 a. homo
         b. sapiens
2.25 blood
2.26 fertile
2.27 d
2.28 f
2.29 g
2.30 c
2.31 b

2.32 They received similar genetic material from their parents.
2.33 a. interaction between a pair of alleles
         b. interaction with their environment
2.34 combinations of
2.35 Any order:
         a. population
         b. environment
         c. common language
2.36 language
2.37 barrier
2.38 intramarriage

SELF TEST 2

2.01 c
2.02 e
2.03 g
2.04 i
2.05 k
2.06 m
2.07 o
2.08 a
2.09 n
2.010 l
2.011 j
2.012 h
2.013 f
2.014 d
2.015 b
2.016 comparative
2.017 Any order:
a. Japhetites
b. Semites
c. Hamites
2.018 dust
2.019 participant observation
2.020 Any order:
a. population
b. environment
c. language
2.021 everlasting
2.022 a. conscious
b. responsibility
2.023 Any three:
a. death
b. birth
c. puberty
or marriage
2.024 God
2.025 __6__
2.026 __5__
2.027 __1__
2.028 __7__
2.029 __3__
2.030 __2__
2.031 __4__
2.032 b
2.033 c
2.034 b
2.035 a

SECTION 3

3.1 ACROSS
1. deplete
2. alliance
3. lifestyle
4. intermarriage
DOWN
1. durable
2. clan
3. alkaloid
4. inherent
3.2 b
3.3 d
3.4 f
3.5 h
3.6 j
3.7 i
3.8 g
3.9 e
3.10 c
3.11 a
3.12 cultural
3.13 Either order:
a. hunting
b. gathering
3.14 move
3.15 dry
3.16 possessions
3.17 Either order:
a. horticulture
b. hunting
3.18 protection
3.19 move
3.20 a. Hopi
b. wind-blown
3.21 rain
3.22 true
3.23 false
3.24 false
3.25 true
3.26 true
3.27 b. They must move their herds to new grazing land
3.28 The following items must be checked:
✓ food
✓ fuel
✓ grooming supplies
✓ wall plaster
3.29 a. dry
b. rains
c. scattered.

3.30 Any of the following:
It is made from local materials.
It protects against the wind and cold.
It lasts the whole season.

3.31 Any of the following:
It gives protection from the sun and wind.
It gives protection from the cold.
It can be built quickly.

3.32 b, c

3.33 a, d

3.34 a, d

3.35 d

3.36 kin

3.37 intermarriage

3.38 kinship

3.39 a. weaker
b. stronger

3.40 battles

3.41 Examples:
To have success in life; to have supernatural ability.

3.42 through visions

3.43 Example:
Some came unsought; through a form of ordeal.

3.44 Example:
By singing a certain song; by wearing something special on his head.

3.45 Magic

3.46 The Pilgrim's method provided nutriments used by the corn; the Azande's method provided nothing the corn could use.

3.47 Both are relying on a supernatural force to grow a good crop.

3.48 arrow

3.49 b. reading signs

3.50 c. omens

3.51 d. yes/no

3.52 a. rubbing board

3.53 d. poison

3.54 Teacher check
Bible verses listed:
Read Deuteronomy 18:10-12;
1 Samuel 15:23; Proverbs 16:33;
Joshua 7:13; Numbers 26:55;
1 Samuel 10:20; Acts 1:26
Example:
God forbids the use of divination. Its use is an abomination unto the Lord.

SELF TEST 3

3.01 b

3.02 d

3.03 f

3.04 h

3.05 j

3.06 l

3.07 a

3.08 n

3.09 o

3.010 m

3.011 k

3.012 i

3.013 g

3.014 e

3.015 c

3.016 d. laboratories

3.017 b. one year

3.018 c. comparative method

3.019 d. in God's image

3.020 b. protection

3.021 a. nomadic

3.022 c. few possessions

3.023 b. science

3.024 a. magic

3.025 a. magic

3.026 d. local materials

3.027 b. relativism

3.028 subdue

3.029 Homo sapiens

3.030 language

3.031 marriage

3.032 Pastoral

3.033 divination

3.034 Any three:
a. death
b. birth
c. puberty
or marriage

3.035 a. environment
b. language

3.036 true

3.037 true

3.038 false

3.039 false

3.040 false

3.041 true

LIFEPAC TEST

1. b
2. d
3. f
4. h
5. j
6. i
7. g
8. e
9. c
10. a
11. c. God
12. c. subdue his environment
13. d. environments differ
14. b. food, protection, and prosperity
15. c
16. e
17. g
18. i
19. a
20. j
21. h
22. f
23. d
24. b
25. a
26. a
27. _7_
28. _2_
29. _4_
30. _6_
31. _5_
32. _1_
33. _3_
34. a, d
35. b, c
36. a, d
37. c
38. a, d
39. a, d
40. regularities
41. comparative
42. participant observation
43. monograph

ALTERNATE LIFEPAC TEST

1. c
2. b
3. a
4. d
5. c
6. c
7. a
8. b
9. a
10. d
11. false
12. false
13. true
14. true
15. false
16. true
17. true
18. false
19. false
20. true
21. past
22. Eve
23. dust
24. Shem
25. Babel
26. gene
27. Hamites
28. igloo
29. image
30. diary
31. d
32. g
33. a
34. i
35. e
36. h
37. f
38. b
39. k
40. j

HISTORY & GEOGRAPHY 704

ALTERNATE LIFEPAC TEST

NAME _____

DATE _____

SCORE _____

64

80

Write the letter for the correct answer on each line (each answer, 2 points).

1. Anthropology is the study of _____ .
    a. animals   b. birds   c. man   d. religion

2. Culture is the way man _____ his environment.
    a. submits   b. subdues   c. submerges   d. substitutes

3. The cultural regularity discovered by Arnold van Gennep was _____ .
    a. rites of passage b. folklore   c. kin-groups   d. toolmaking

4. Seeing foreign cultures as inferior to one's own is known as _____ .
    a. game   b. superiority   c. nonliterate   d. ethnocentrism

5. *Culture shock* is a form of _____ .
    a. violence   b. anthropology   c. trauma   d. travel

6. The principal task of the field worker in anthropology is to gather _____ .
    a. tribes   b. kinships   c. information   d. berries

7. The type of anthropologist who goes out to study living tribes is know as a(n) _____ .
    a. ethnographer   b. archaeologist   c. sage   d. sociologist

8. Man is classed by scientists as belonging to the genus *Homo* and species _____ .
    a. pithecanthropus b. sapiens   c. human   d. taxa

9. The number of bones in the human body is _____ .
    a. 206   b. 52   c. 12   d. 100

10. To anthropologists, human groups are like _____ .
    a. tools   b. cultures   c. societies   d. laboratories

Answer *true* **or** *false* (each answer, 1 point).

11. _____ Anthropology courses are not important for doing fieldwork.

12. _____ An anthropologist knows nothing about a group of people before living with them.

13. _____ Anthropologists often have difficulty adjusting to a new way of life.

14. _____ Words are sounds that have a specific meaning.

15. _____ Mankind has never had a common language.

16. _____ Clear communication helps a society stay together.

17. _____ Every society has a meaningful language.

18. _____ Adam had six sons whose descendants spread out across the world from Babel.

19. _____ Horticulturists grow cattle and other livestock.

20. _____ The source of all creation is God.

Complete these sentences (each answer, 3 points).

21. Archaeologists are interest in man's _____ .

22. The mother of all people was _____ .

23. The bodies of all people are composed of common elements described in the Bible as

_____ .

24. The three sons of Noah were Ham, Japheth, and _____ .

25. The Lord confused the language of people in the city of _____ .

26. Each parent contributes one *allele* for every _____ in a child.

27. The three races associated with the descendants of Noah are the Japhetites, Semites, and

_____ .

28. An Inuit house made of blocks of hard snow is called a(n) _____ .

29. According to the Bible (Genesis 1:27), "...God created man in His own _____ ."

30. A field worker in anthropology should keep a daily _____ .

Match these items (each answer, 2 points).

31.	_____ list of marriages, births, deaths, and so forth	a. Branislaw Malinowski
32.	_____ reveals inner feelings	b. holistic
33.	_____ began training ethnographers	c. monograph
34.	_____ feast where wealth is given away	d. census
35.	_____ group of related families	e. clan
36.	_____ having two feet; walking upright	f. trauma
37.	_____ shock	g. psychological test
38.	_____ study every aspect of culture	h. bipedal
39.	_____ a view that one's own culture is superior	i. potlatch
40.	_____ digs up ancient ruins	j. archaeologist
		k. ethnocentric

HISTORY & GEOGRAPHY 705

Unit 5: Sociology—Man In Groups

TEACHER NOTES

MATERIALS NEEDED FOR LIFEPAC	
Required	Suggested
None	• atlas • encyclopedia • reference books or online sources

ADDITIONAL LEARNING ACTIVITIES

Section 1: An Introduction to Sociology

1. Discuss these questions with your class.

   a. How are sociology and psychology different? Who does the sociologist work with? Who does the psychologist work with? Invite a sociologist or a psychologist to visit the class and answer students' questions.

   b. Discuss a perfect society. How would a utopia differ from the society we have today? Can any society be completely perfect?

2. Have partners describe their nuclear family. Then have them describe their extended family. Which turned out to be longer? Why?

3. Discuss socialization with your group. Why do some people grow up to be responsible and productive Christians while others choose to stay on sinful paths?

4. Assign students to write a brief report on propaganda and its uses. In the report, they must address the question, is advertising a form of propaganda?

5. Ask students, what is a fad? Have you ever taken part in one? Are you still enthusiastic about it? What do sociologists say about fads?

Section 2: The Method of Sociology

1. Show the class some statistical charts or graphs and explain how they are used and what they mean. Have students ask as many questions as they can based on the charts and graphs.

2. Obtain a copy of Alexis de Tocqueville's famous book *Democracy in America*, written in the 19th century, and read aloud certain brief passages of his observations on life in the United States. Digital copies are available online. Are his observations still true today? Discuss why or why not.

3. Have students visit the home of a friend, and with permission, write a brief case study of what they find there, as if they were a sociologist. If possible, the friend could return the visit and write a brief case study. The two compare their case studies.

4. Have each student think of three questions and conduct a random sampling of the class based on those questions. For example, a student might ask each person their favorite sport. Have the class discuss what conclusions they can draw from the surveys.

5. Clip the results of a recent poll such as the Gallup Poll from a newspaper or online source. Discuss as a class: What questions did it ask? How were the answers distributed? How would you have answered the questions?

6. Assign students to write a brief report on the lives of Durkheim, Weber, Sumner, or one of the other classical sociologists. The report should address these questions: How did he look at society? For what is he especially remembered?

Administer the LIFEPAC Test

The test is to be administered in one session. Give no help except with directions.
Evaluate the tests and review areas where the students have done poorly.
Review the pages and activities that stress the concepts tested.
If necessary, administer the Alternate LIFEPAC Test.

ANSWER KEYS

SECTION 1

1.1	b
1.2	d
1.3	f
1.4	h
1.5	g
1.6	e
1.7	c
1.8	a
1.9	true
1.10	true
1.11	false
1.12	true
1.13	true
1.14	false
1.15	true
1.16	true

1.17 ACROSS
1. diffusion
2. ethnocentrism
3. folkway
4. mores
5. positivism

DOWN
6. futurology
7. propaganda
8. socialization
9. utopia
10. epistemology

1.18 Groups are composed of individuals, which in turn, are influenced by the group.

1.19 Economics is the study of the production of goods and services.

1.20 Either order:
a. physical
b. cultural

1.21 Anthropology is the science that studies man.

1.22	c
1.23	e
1.24	f
1.25	d
1.26	a
1.27	b

1.28 social psychology

1.29 the origin and development of the different races of man

1.30	b
1.31	a
1.32	c
1.33	c
1.34	d
1.35	a
1.36	b

1.37 Either order:
a. church
b. family

1.38 evolution
1.39 determinism
1.40 communism
1.41 A group is a set of people who are joined together by common interests.

1.42 a. institution
b. association
c. association
d. institution
e. association

1.43 a. S
b. P
c. P
d. P
e. S
f. S

1.44 Answers could include: family—primary; church—primary; city—secondary

1.45 Culture is all the ways of thinking and acting that a person acquires from society.

1.46 It comes from our training as we grow up.
1.47 an Englishman
1.48 through language
1.49 Any order:
a. gestures
b. laughter
c. songs
d. military symbols
e. bells
f. processions
g. crosses
h. caps and gowns

1.50 Cultural accumulation is when one culture gradually takes on the culture of another society.

1.51 Cultural diffusion is the spread of traits from one culture to many other cultures.

1.52 Folkways

1.53 Mores

1.54 Ethnocentrism is when one culture is believed to be better than all others.

1.55 socialization

1.56 self-control

1.57 individual

1.58 Either order:
a. emotional
b. physical

1.59 life goals

1.60 self

1.61 loved

1.62 true

1.63 Either order:
a. getting up in the morning
b. delaying gratification

1.64 Any order:
a. writing letters
b. talking with new acquaintances
c. using table manners

1.65 Collective behavior is behavior associated with relatively unorganized groups of people.

1.66 Examples:
race riot, football game, fads

1.67 Emotional contagion is a shared or common emotional mood or experience.

1.68 A rumor is an unconfirmed or unfounded communication.

1.69 Public opinion is a shared opinion on some issue.

1.70 The aim of propaganda is to use the media to influence public opinion.

1.71 a. Christian groups are social.
b. Christians can better understand their influence in a group.
c. Christianity does affect culture.

1.72 a. where people live
b. how many people move in or out of an area
c. how many people die and are born in an area

SELF TEST 1

1.01 e

1.02 j

1.03 g

1.04 d

1.05 a

1.06 b

1.07 k

1.08 c

1.09 f

1.010 h

1.011 Either order:
a. physical
b. cultural

1.012 groups

1.013 kingdom

1.014 Either order:
a. church
b. family

1.015 institution

1.016 primary

1.017 family

1.018 secondary

1.019 culture

1.020 acquired

1.021 diffusion

1.022 individual

1.023 true

1.024 true

1.025 true

1.026 true

1.027 true

1.028 true

1.029 false

1.030 true

1.031 a. S
b. P
c. P
d. P
e. S
f. S

1.032 Any order:
a. population studies
b. social groups
c. cultural influences
d. social changes
e. social behavior

SECTION 2

2.1	e
2.2	a
2.3	c
2.4	f
2.5	d
2.6	b
2.7	a. society
	b. aspect
	c. pattern
2.8	suicide
2.9	static
2.10	false
2.11	Sociological description is the use of words to tell how something actually happened.
2.12	a. Alexis de Tocqueville
	b. *Democracy in America*
2.13	idealized
2.14	In the statistical approach, data is collected and used to test hypotheses.
2.15	A hypothesis is the possible answer or approach to a problem.
2.16	Probability is the possibility that something is true or valid.
2.17	Statistical analysis is called the historical method because collected data can be concerned with what has already occurred.
2.18	A sociological survey involves interviews to obtain relevant facts.
2.19	A selected sample is a representative group.
2.20	A random sample is something chosen by chance.
2.21	a. statistical
	b. description
2.22	b. small
2.23	a. an indication
2.24	Any order:
	a. by age
	b. by religion
	c. by education level
	d. by race
	e. by sex
2.25	Any order:
	a. description
	b. statistics
	c. survey
	d. experiment
	e. participant observation
2.26	Field
2.27	case
2.28	Teacher check

SELF TEST 2

2.01	c
2.02	e
2.03	a
2.04	g
2.05	f
2.06	d
2.07	b
2.08	b. sociology
2.09	a. anthropology
2.010	d. history
2.011	b. psychology
2.012	c. political science
2.013	hypothesis
2.014	theorists
2.015	society
2.016	description
2.017	*Democracy in America*
2.018	a. specific
	b. theories
2.019	research
2.020	a. data
	b. hypothesis
2.021	Probability
2.022	survey
2.023	sampling
2.024	random
2.025	Either order:
	a. family
	b. church
2.026	the family
2.027	A primary group is a close association of persons and is characterized by personal contact, mutual dependence, and total involvement.
2.028	true
2.029	true
2.030	false
2.031	true
2.032	a. description
	b. statistics
	c. controlled experiments
	d. surveys
	e. field observation

LIFEPAC TEST

1. f
2. a
3. i
4. k
5. e
6. o
7. c
8. b
9. j
10. d
11. g
12. h
13. m
14. l
15. true
16. false
17. false
18. true
19. true
20. true
21. false
22. true
23. true
24. true
25. false
26. true
27. false
28. true
29. false
30. group
31. Philosophy
32. diffusion
33. culture
34. probability
35. Either order:
    a. physical
    b. cultural
36. culture
37. discipline
38. emotional
39. emotional
40. rumor
41. government
42. c
43. a
44. b
45. b
46. c
47. a
48. d
49. b
50. Teacher check

ALTERNATE LIFEPAC TEST

1. f
2. c
3. i
4. b
5. j
6. k
7. g
8. a
9. e
10. d
11. true
12. true
13. true
14. true
15. false
16. true
17. false
18. false
19. false
20. false
21. suicide
22. Plato
23. past
24. survey
25. primary
26. man
27. case study
28. God
29. public
30. future
31. c
32. a
33. b
34. b
35. c
36. d
37. a
38. a
39. d
40. c

HISTORY & GEOGRAPHY 705

ALTERNATE LIFEPAC TEST

NAME _____

DATE _____

SCORE _____

64
80

Match these items (each answer, 2 points).

1.	_____ sociology	a.	set of people with a common interest
2.	_____ Marx and Engels	b.	ideal society
3.	_____ probability	c.	economic determinists
4.	_____ utopia	d.	group that serves a public purpose
5.	_____ diffusion	e.	information
6.	_____ socialization	f.	the study of society
7.	_____ propaganda	g.	influences public opinion
8.	_____ group	h.	shared emotion
9.	_____ data	i.	likelihood
10.	_____ institution	j.	spread of a cultural trait
		k.	makes an individual part of society

Answer *true* **or** *false* (each answer, 1 point).

11. _____ The nuclear family refers to father, mother, brothers, and sisters.

12. _____ Auguste Comte was the "father of sociology."

13. _____ Folkways are long-held customs.

14. _____ A fad is an example of collective behavior.

15. _____ Culture is hereditary.

16. _____ Herbert Spencer attempted to apply the theory of biological evolution to sociology.

17. _____ When a culture believes it is worse than all others, it is called ethnocentric.

18. _____ The most obvious example of a secondary group is the family.

19. _____ Sociology is concerned with individuals and not groups.

20. _____ The process through which an individual is made a part of society is called emotional contagion.

Complete these sentences (each answer, 3 points).

21. Emile Durkheim, the first scientific sociologist, was famous for his scientific study of

_____ .

22. The Greek philosopher who imagined a completely planned, perfect society was

_____ .

23. History is the study of man's _____ .

24. Random sampling is a general type of _____ .

25. A group in which members have close, personal contact is a _____ group.

26. Anthropology is the study of _____ .

27. A report made by a sociologist from field observations is called a(n) _____

_____ .

28. In the Scripture, the ideal society is the kingdom of _____ .

29. A shared opinion on a political or some other issue is called _____ opinion.

30. Futurology studies society's present and past to determine where it is headed in the

_____ .

Write the letter for the correct answer on each line (each answer, 2 points).

31. The immediate family is the _____ family.
    a. extended   b. cultural   c. nuclear   d. social

32. Grandparents, aunts, uncles, and cousins to which the nuclear family is related are the _____ family.
    a. extended   b. cultural   c. social   d. primary

33. Sociology deals with _____ rather than individuals.
    a. pairs   b. groups   c. families   d. utopias

34. The study of individual behavior is called _____ .
    a. economics   b. psychology   c. philosophy   d. sociology

35. Plato's society was the first of many _____ .
    a. city-states   b. republics   c. utopias   d. dictatorships

36. The basis for present-day communism was provided by _____ .
    a. Weber   b. Durkheim   c. Comte   d. Marx

37. Asking people about themselves and their attitudes is known as a(n) _____ .
    a. survey   b. quiz   c. hypothesis   d. data

38. Controlled experiments are used to give _____ of a group's reaction.
    a. an indication   b. a theory   c. a final conclusion   d. a guess

39. Two kinds of anthropology are cultural and _____ .
    a. mathematical   b. psychological   c. biased   d. physical

40. Culture is _____ , not inherited.
    a. collective   b. diffused   c. learned   d. spoken

HISTORY & GEOGRAPHY 706

Unit 6: U.S. Anthropology and Sociology

TEACHER NOTES

MATERIALS NEEDED FOR LIFEPAC	
Required	Suggested
None	• map of North America • encyclopedia • reference books or online sources

ADDITIONAL LEARNING ACTIVITIES

Section 1: Cultural Background of the United States

1. Collect and display pictures and information of the various Native American cultures. Emphasize diversity of cultures and close relationship to natural environment.

2. Discuss false or prejudicial ideas about Native Americans and their way of life, such as "Inuits live in igloos" or "Indians are better hunters." Discuss why prejudice is harmful and wrong.

3. Arrange for a class visit to a museum having Native American artifacts or to a Native American cultural center. If this is not possible, you find displays or videos on museum websites.

4. Have students research the Northwest Native American potlatch as well as the customs, foods, and beliefs of these people groups. Students can make a presentation or write paragraphs to answer these questions: What types of gifts would be given away? What would the physical setting be like?

5. Have students select several Native American tribes from different regions and compare the ways in which they handled *one* of these phases of life:

    a. food gathering and preservation

    b. personal adornment

    c. controlling bad behavior of tribal members

    d. caring for and educating children

    e. celebrations and recreation

    f. religious beliefs

    g. trade with other tribes

    Assign students a written or oral report on their findings.

6. Have students report on one of the present-day controversies over Native American rights to land, fish, oil, irrigation water, police authority, or political power. Students should propose possible solutions in the report.

Section 2: Sociology and Culture Groups from Distant Lands

1. Make sure students understand the immigration quota system, its rationale, present requirements, and control system. Discuss these quotas in light of current pressures such as illegal immigration from Mexico and other countries, refugees from Southeast Asia and other regions, and any related debates.

2. Discuss with the class examples of harmful stereotyping of national, racial, or occupational groups. Emphasize Christian responsibility in this area. Use local and current examples.

3. If possible, have a naturalized citizen from another country speak to the class about their reasons for coming to America, experiences as an immigrant, and the process of becoming a citizen. An interview could also be found online.

4. Tabulate the countries from which the ancestors of class members came to America. Have the class plot these by pins placed on an outline map of the world. Remind students that most people in America have several national ties, and that not everyone can be sure of their origins because family records are not complete.

5. If your community has any ethnic restaurants, obtain menus and find out about the ingredients of unfamiliar foods. If possible, make a class visit or have someone prepare one dish so that everyone can taste it.

6. Have students do a more thorough research study on one ethnic group or group of people and their immigration or presence in America. Have students report to class.

7. The Statue of Liberty is the symbol of America's welcome to all peoples. Assign students to make a special report on its history and symbolism.

8. Tell students the following for a sharing activity: If your family has a special object, such as a picture, plate, basket, or piece of clothing brought to this country from their former home, ask if you may bring it to class. Remember that such items are irreplaceable, and take good care of it.

9. The idea of social classes is often resisted by Americans. Discuss the social classes, their values, problems, and distinguishing characteristics. Emphasize that God does not consider social class important and that all classes share a common humanity.

Section 3: Cultural and Social Interaction

1. Discuss urbanization and its effects on American economic life, the family, and the church.

2. Instruct groups to prepare a report on the changes in your own community in the past fifty years. Students should make committees to divide up the work. Some students should interview older people in the community and others should collect information from the library or online resources.

3. As a class, debate the advantages of rural life over city life or vice versa.

4. As a class, collect and display photos with examples of body language and gestures. Examples should also be from other cultures.

5. Tell students to look at the list of cultural changes brought about by refrigeration in the LIFEPAC. Have the class develop a similar list based on another technological change, such as mobile phones, central heating, computers, or the internet.

6. Have students write a brief account on a tradition in their family, such as a special way of celebrating birthdays, a typical Thanksgiving, or an annual visit to a favorite vacation spot. Students should discuss with family members to see how this tradition was started.

Administer the LIFEPAC Test

The test is to be administered in one session. Give no help except with directions.
Evaluate the tests and review areas where the students have done poorly.
Review the pages and activities that stress the concepts tested.
If necessary, administer the Alternate LIFEPAC Test.

ANSWER KEYS

SECTION 1

1.1 ACROSS
1. adze
2. artifact
3. awl
4. breechcloth
5. emigrate
6. glacier
7. indigenous
8. leggings

DOWN
9. extinct
10. fowl
11. absolute
12. belief
13. custom

1.2 b
1.3 d
1.4 f
1.5 h
1.6 j
1.7 l
1.8 k
1.9 i
1.10 g
1.11 e
1.12 c
1.13 a
1.14 archaeologists
1.15 nomads
1.16 extinct
1.17 migrated
1.18 Bering Strait
1.19 c
1.20 e
1.21 g
1.22 a
1.23 h
1.24 f
1.25 d
1.26 b
1.27 Any order:
a. Algonquian
b. Iroquoian
1.28 Any order:
a. bone
b. stone
c. wood

1.29 a. W
b. B
c. W
d. L
e. L
1.30 b. to keep intruders out
1.31 Any order:
a. squash
b. beans
c. pumpkin
d. corn
e. tobacco
1.32 wampum
1.33 a. League
b. Hiawatha
1.34 Confederacy
1.35 c. women
1.36 b. English
1.37 Any order:
a. Cayuga
b. Mohawk
c. Oneida
d. Onondaga
e. Seneca
1.38 Tuscaroras
1.39 a. Natchez
b. Mobiles
c. Wacos
d. Creeks
1.40 Cahokia
1.41 a. fruit
b. baskets
c. pearls
1.42 salt
1.43 Cherokee
1.44 diseases
1.45 false
1.46 true
1.47 true
1.48 false
1.49 true
1.50 false
1.51 true
1.52 false

1.53 pueblos
1.54 a. _X_
b. ___
c. _X_
d. _X_
e. ___
f. ___
g. _X_
h. _X_
1.55 a. ___
b. _X_
c. _X_
d. _X_
e. _X_
f. _X_
g. ___
1.56 a. _X_
b. ___
c. _X_
d. ___
e. _X_
1.57 a. ___
b. _X_
c. ___
d. _X_
e. _X_
f. ___
g. ___
1.58 a. _X_
b. ___
c. _X_
d. ___
e. ___
f. ___
g. _X_
h. _X_
i. _X_
j. _X_
1.59 lamps
1.60 raw meat
1.61 a. _X_
b. _X_
c. ___
d. ___
e. ___
f. _X_
g. _X_
h. ___

1.62 Either order:
a. Marquesas Islands
b. Tahiti
1.63 a. M
b. C
c. W
d. M
e. W
f. W
1.64 a. _X_
b. ___
c. _X_
d. ___
e. _X_
f. ___
g. _X_
h. _X_
i. _X_
j. ___
1.65 king
1.66 Teacher check

SELF TEST 1

1.01	b
1.02	d
1.03	f
1.04	g
1.05	a
1.06	e
1.07	c
1.08	true
1.09	false
1.010	false
1.011	true
1.012	false
1.013	false
1.014	false
1.015	false
1.016	false
1.017	true
1.018	c
1.019	c
1.020	b
1.021	a
1.022	a
1.023	b
1.024	a
1.025	c
1.026	c
1.027	b
1.028	d
1.029	a
1.030	c
1.031	c
1.032	b
1.033	buffalo
1.034	Hawaii
1.035	Spanish
1.036	potlatch
1.037	Bering Strait
1.038	raw meat

SECTION 2

2.1	c
2.2	e
2.3	g
2.4	i
2.5	a
2.6	h
2.7	f
2.8	d
2.9	b
2.10	immigrants
2.11	Anglo-Saxons
2.12	Germans
2.13	Pennsylvania Dutch
2.14	Italians
2.15	true
2.16	true
2.17	false
2.18	true
2.19	true
2.20	g
2.21	d
2.22	i
2.23	a
2.24	h
2.25	b
2.26	k
2.27	c
2.28	f
2.29	l
2.30	Hawaii
2.31	Gold Hill
2.32	false
2.33	false
2.34	true
2.35	true
2.36	true
2.37	true
2.38	Teacher check
2.39	c
2.40	e
2.41	b
2.42	f
2.43	d
2.44	a
2.45	true
2.46	true
2.47	false
2.48	true
2.49	true
2.50	true

2.51 Any order:
   a. Buddhism
   b. Hinduism
   c. Islam
   d. Christianity
   e. Judaism
2.52 one-sixth
2.53 ghettos
2.54 Any order:
   a. upper
   b. middle
   c. poor
2.55 Any order:
   a. money
   b. occupation
   c. education

SELF TEST 2

2.01 true
2.02 false
2.03 true
2.04 false
2.05 false
2.06 false
2.07 true
2.08 true
2.09 false
2.010 f
2.011 a
2.012 e
2.013 d
2.014 c
2.015 c. work in the gold mines
2.016 a. can be harmful to individuals
2.017 a. when fuel was scarce
2.018 b. Hawaiian
2.019 c. around Lancaster, Pennsylvania
2.020 c. they lived in different environments
2.021 d
2.022 h
2.023 j
2.024 g
2.025 k
2.026 i
2.027 c
2.028 e
2.029 a
2.030 f
2.031 Any order:
   a. Sweden
   b. Finland
   c. Norway
   d. Denmark
2.032 Japanese
2.033 Russians
2.034 Any order:
   a. Central America
   b. South America
   c. Mexico
2.035 Louisiana
2.036 b
2.037 d
2.038 f
2.039 a
2.040 e
2.041 c

SECTION 3

3.1   a. ___
       b. ___
       c. ✓
       d. ___
       e. ___
       f. ✓
3.2   c
3.3   d
3.4   a
3.5   b
3.6   technology
3.7   machines
3.8   industrialized
3.9   false
3.10 Any order:
       a. family
       b. education
       c. religion
       d. government
       e. economic
3.11 Stable
3.12 school
3.13 industrialization
3.14 assimilation
3.15 true
3.16 false
3.17 true
3.18 true
3.19 true
3.20 jobs
3.21 urbanization
3.22 values
3.23 roles
3.24 isolated
3.25 class
3.26 Either order:
       a. Poor people are left in central cities.
       b. More cars are needed.
3.27 older
3.28 Any order:
       a. Who will earn the money?
       b. Who will cook the food?
       c. Adults have less time for each other.

SELF TEST 3

3.01 false
3.02 true
3.03 true
3.04 false
3.05 true
3.06 false
3.07 false
3.08 true
3.09 a. value
3.010 b. fewer people were needed to grow food
3.011 d. a, b, and c
3.012 c. isolated
3.013 c. their ties to their homeland were damaged
3.014 b. tools and machinery
3.015 c. home language
3.016 d. Jewish
3.017 b. Germans
3.018 a. Russians
3.019 Any order:
       a. economic
       b. government
       c. religion
3.020 Irish
3.021 diseases
3.022 a. homes
       b. shops
3.023 a. Asia
       b. Bering Strait
3.024 Any order:
       a. money
       b. education
       c. occupation
3.025 buffalo
3.026 English
3.027 industrialized
3.028 Any order:
       a. Buddhism
       b. Hinduism
       c. Islam
       d. Judaism
       e. Christianity
3.029 assimilation
3.030 bilingual
3.031 technology
3.032 urbanization

LIFEPAC TEST

1. true
2. false
3. true
4. false
5. true
6. true
7. true
8. false
9. true
10. false
11. dialect
12. Any order:
    a. English (England)
    b. Scots (Scotland)
    c. Welsh (Wales)
13. a. pierced
    b. tattooed
14. b
15. c
16. a
17. language
18. Any two:
    a. Chinese
    b. Japanese
    or Native American
       Russians
19. melting pot
20. Cherokee
21. Any order:
    a. upper
    b. middle
    c. lower
22. c
23. g
24. h
25. e
26. a
27. j
28. f
29. d
30. k
31. b
32. d. a, b, and c
33. d. a, b, and c
34. c. isolated
35. a. different
36. c. pemmican
37. b. Jews
38. a. the family
39. d. Irish

ALTERNATE LIFEPAC TEST

1. true
2. true
3. true
4. false
5. true
6. false
7. false
8. true
9. true
10. true
11. Examples; any order:
    a. love
    b. belonging
    c. sense of achievement
    or beauty
       fulfillment
12. Any order:
    a. home
    b. school
    c. church
13. Any three:
    a. Martin Luther King's birthday
    b. Lincoln's birthday
    c. Washington's birthday
    or Groundhog Day
       Arbor Day
       Pulaski's birthday
       Mother's Day
       Father's Day
       Memorial Day
       Flag Day
       Independence Day
       Labor Day
       Columbus Day
14. an increase in city living
15. melting
16. Any three:
    a. Hopi
    b. Navajo
    c. Apache
    or Zuni
       Pima
       Papago
17. Any three:
    a. Geronimo
    b. Cochise
    c. Crazy Horse
18. Any order:
    a. money
    b. occupation
    c. education

19. Examples; any order:
    a. family
    b. schools
    c. churches
    or businesses
20. Any three:
    a. strength
    b. direction
    c. faith
    or support
       peace of mind
21. f
22. e
23. d
24. h
25. j
26. a
27. b
28. g
29. i
30. c
31. c. pluralistic
32. b. hunting and fishing
33. c. family
34. d. both a. and b.
35. d. interpersonal relationships
36. a. assimilated many useful things
37. c. Christian tradition
38. b. slavery prevented communication and
    broke up many black families

HISTORY & GEOGRAPHY 706

ALTERNATE LIFEPAC TEST

NAME _____

DATE _____

SCORE _____

99
124

Answer *true* or *false* (each answer, 1 point).

1. _____ People can be grouped by age, national origin, geography, and in many other ways.

2. _____ The early inhabitants of the Hawaiian Islands were Polynesians who came from Marquesas, another island group.

3. _____ People from England, Scotland, and Wales were the first major group of white settlers along the Atlantic seaboard.

4. _____ Very few immigrants came to America from Italy.

5. _____ Native Americans believed land was to be used well, but not owned.

6. _____ Inuits used only the best meat from seals and whales and discarded the rest of the carcasses.

7. _____ The most important game animal for the Plains Indians was the moose.

8. _____ Potlatch celebrations were part of the culture of the Native American people in the Northwest Coast.

9. _____ The early nomads who settled North America probably came across the Bering Strait to what is now Alaska.

10. _____ Many immigrant groups were subjected to prejudice and discrimination in this country.

Complete these statements (each answer, 3 points).

11. Three basic psychological needs of all people are a. _____ ,

    b. _____ , and c. _____ .

12. Three important educational institutions are the a. _____ ,

    b. _____ , and c. _____ .

13. Three holidays celebrated *only* in the United States are a. _____ ,

    b. _____ , and c. _____ .

14. *Urbanization* means _____ .

15. Because the United States has absorbed people, customs, and languages from many

    countries and cultures, we call it a _____ pot.

16. Three tribes of Native Americans that live in the Southwest are the

    a. _____ , b. _____ , and c. _____ .

17. Three famous Native American leaders were a. _____ ,

    b. _____ , and c. _____ .

18. Social class in America is determined largely by a. _____ ,

    b. _____ , and c. _____ .

19. Three basic institutions in all societies are a. _____ ,

    b. _____ , and c. _____ .

20. When religion is a dominant force in a person's life, it gives the individual

    a. _____ , b. _____ , and c. _____ .

Match these items (each answer, 2 points).

21. _____ Mormons
22. _____ body language
23. _____ Sequoyah
24. _____ ethnic
25. _____ Japanese
26. _____ assimilation
27. _____ Estevanico
28. _____ travois
29. _____ artifact
30. _____ bilingual

a. the merging of elements from two or more cultures into one
b. black explorer of the Southwest
c. able to speak two languages
d. invented a written Cherokee language
e. facial expressions, postures, or movements which convey meaning
f. religious group that settled in Utah
g. device made of poles for dragging supplies
h. based on nationality or race
i. physical remains of a culture, such as tools
j. one of the groups of immigrants from Asia
k. masks worn by Native American dancers

Write the letter for the correct answer on each line (each answer, 2 points).

31. American society, composed of many different national groups, is a _____ society.
    a. monopolistic   b. chauvinistic   c. pluralistic   d. communistic

32. Inuit survival was based on _____ .
    a. inherited wealth   b. hunting and fishing
    c. agriculture   d. trade with many other groups

33. The institution in society that satisfies most of the individual's psychological needs is the
    _____ .
    a. government   b. neighborhood   c. family   d. school

34. An example of technological change that has deeply affected society is _____ .
    a. the automobile   b. television   c. rainfall   d. both a. and b.

35. Rural life usually provides more _____ than city life does.
    a. employment   b. commercial entertainment
    c. class distinction   d. interpersonal relationships

36. When they encountered the Native American cultures, the white men _____ .
    a. assimilated many useful things   b. went back to Europe
    c. established no contacts   d. changed completely to Native American ways

37. Mardi Gras is a holiday based on _____ .
    a. the Buddhist religion
    b. the Jewish religion
    c. Christian tradition
    d. French independence celebration

38. Black people have not kept up strong connections with their original cultures in Africa because _____ .
    a. they came too late
    b. slavery prevented communication and broke up many black families
    c. they preferred American ways
    d. they tried to forget their old ways

HISTORY & GEOGRAPHY 707

Unit 7: Economics—Resources and Need

TEACHER NOTES

MATERIALS NEEDED FOR LIFEPAC	
Required	Suggested
None	• dictionary • encyclopedia • almanac • Bible • reference books or online sources

ADDITIONAL LEARNING ACTIVITIES

Section 1: What is Economics?

1. Hold class discussion on *wants* and *needs*. Use specific examples from student experience. Include the question: Can one person's want be another person's need?

2. To illustrate the difference between simple and complex societies, discuss and list in two columns on the board the ways in which American pioneers and contemporary Americans have obtained the following items: food, clothing, living quarters for families, medical care, transportation of goods, and exchange of news.

3. Using a specific commodity such as coffee or shoes, have the class analyze factors which might affect supply, such as weather, shipping charges, or labor shortages and those which might affect demand, such as population increases, fashion, social customs, or reported health hazards.

4. Divide the class into four groups: factory workers, factory owners, distributors, and consumers. Have each group present its view to the whole class. Question: Should the price of the finished product, such as a pair of shoes, be increased when raw material, such as leather, go up in price?

5. Have students list all the foods on the school lunch menu for one day. Then, tell them to list the people and machines involved in producing each food and getting it to the lunchroom table. This example shows a complex society in action.

6. Arrange a field trip to a large farm, factory, or warehouse to get some idea of what is involved in production and distribution of goods. If possible, find out the cost of producing and distributing each unit.

7. Have students choose a primitive society of the past. Instruct them to find out how this group met its basic needs, whether or not any form of money was used, and what commodities a rich person in that society would try to acquire once basic needs had been met. Assign a written or oral report.

8. Instruct students to consult reports in consumer publications in order to find out what typical families spend their money for, and how these expenditures vary with different income levels. Have students develop some graphs to illustrate what they find.

9. Have students list ten less expensive alternatives to the following:

    a. your favorite commercial recreation, such as ball games;

    b. gasoline and travel expenses for trips to the beach, mountains, and so forth; and

    c. your favorite snack or junk food.

Section 2: Methods and Tools of the Economist

1. Bring brochures or printouts of online information from various banks and savings and loan companies to class. Have students compare services and rates of interest. Make sure students understand how money deposited in savings accounts is used to benefit the economy.

2. Discuss taxes, covering the following terms:

    a. What are the taxing bodies in your state and community?

    b. Who determines the level of taxation?

    c. How and what are the most important uses of tax money?

3. Conduct a class money-raising project, such as a popcorn sale or a car wash. Have students keep track of the cost of materials, the hours of labor involved, and the profit made. Ask these questions: How will you determine prices? How many hours of labor went into every $1.00 of profit? Do you consider your project a *financial success*?

4. Tell students to imagine that the class has been given $5,000 to invest. Have different groups do some research and reporting on the following types of investments you might make:

    a. real estate

    b. government saving bonds

    c. a small business such as an answering service or boutique

    d. the stock market

    Students may consult parents and other knowledgeable adults as well as material in the library or online resources.

5. Have students research and report on the life and accomplishments of an outstanding entrepreneur, such as Andrew Carnegie, Henry Ford, Bill Gates, or Steve Jobs.

6. Tell students to watch several commercials for different brands of the same product, such as laundry soap or dog food, and answer these questions: How is the producer trying to appeal to the consumer? Compare prices of the products in the grocery store.

7. Have students read about life in a particular communist or socialist country to see how economic activities such as getting a job, providing a place to live, shopping, and saving are carried on. Ask, how does their life differ from your own family's activities?

Section 3: An Experiment in Economy

1. The concept of goal-setting is an important part of the students' growing self-direction. Discuss how goal-setting is used in athletics, career planning, group activities, and business. Incorporate into the discussion the need to seek God's guidance in selecting goals.

2. Invite a bank loan officer, credit manager, or person who advises families troubled about finances to speak to your class about credit and financial planning. Ask a panel of parents to participate with questions since students may lack the background needed.

3. Have students study online information about different colleges, junior colleges, and technical schools in your area to find out how much a student's yearly expenses would be. Encourage students to Incorporate this information into their long-term goals and financial planning.

4. Hold a class discussion about common consumer frauds. Bring an example and discuss the points that might lead the unwary to lose money.

5. Direct students to interview their pastor or the church financial officer about how church contributions are used, or attend a congregational meeting where church finances will be discussed. Assign them to write a brief report.

6. Provide the following instructions: Choose an item which is a top priority in your financial plan, such as a new bicycle or computer. Investigate the product using consumer publications in the library or online to find out important features and comparative values. Check the current sale price in two or three nearby stores or online retailers. Record useful information and action steps along the way.

7. Provide directions for a follow-up activity: If your family is considering an important purchase, such as a new washing machine, do a similar study on that product and discuss the information with your parents. Ask if you may go along on the buying trip for this item. Write a brief report telling why the particular choice was made.

Administer the LIFEPAC Test

The test is to be administered in one session. Give no help except with directions.
Evaluate the tests and review areas where the students have done poorly.
Review the pages and activities that stress the concepts tested.
If necessary, administer the Alternate LIFEPAC Test.

» ADDITIONAL ACTIVITY ANSWER KEY

SIMPLE SOCIETY	COMPLEX SOCIETY
Spear fishing from a dugout canoe	A fishing trawler with high-powered engine
A storyteller entertaining children	Television
A grass hut	An all-electric ranch house
A corn husk doll	A baby doll that talks when a button is pushed
A man on horseback	A modern car
A hand plow	A large diesel tractor
A drawing on a cave wall	A collection of art in a museum
A lighted candle	An elaborate glass chandelier with electric lights
A bone needle with coarse sinews for thread	An electric sewing machine
A simple trail through the grass or forest	A four-lane highway
A cooking pot over an open fire	Microwave oven

The additional activity on the following two pages may be reproduced as a student worksheet.

» ADDITIONAL ACTIVITY

What type of society is it?

Cut these squares apart and arrange them into two groups, putting those which would be typical of a *simple society* in the first column; those that represent a *complex society* in the second column. Put squares representing similar activities, such as food production, opposite each other.

Spear fishing from a dugout canoe	An electric sewing machine
A storyteller entertaining children	A man on horseback
An elaborate glass chandelier with electric lights	A drawing on a cave wall
A grass hut	A lighted candle
A fishing trawler with high-powered engine	A corn husk doll
A bone needle with coarse sinews for thread	A baby doll that talks when a button is pushed
A modern car	A simple trail through the grass or forest
A cooking pot over an open fire	A hand plow
A large diesel tractor	A four-lane highway
Television	An all-electric ranch style house
A collection of art in a museum	Microwave oven

SIMPLE SOCIETY	COMPLEX SOCIETY

ANSWER KEYS

SECTION 1

1.1   limitless
1.2   Bible
1.3   wants
1.4   needs
1.5   simple
1.6   b
1.7   d
1.8   f
1.9   h
1.10 j
1.11 a
1.12 l
1.13 k
1.14 i
1.15 g
1.16 e
1.17 c
1.18 true
1.19 false
1.20 true
1.21 true
1.22 a
1.23 b
1.24 b
1.25 c
1.26 wants
1.27 free enterprise
1.28 complex
1.29 distributed
1.30 Any order:
   a. What goods and services should be produced.
   b. How goods and services should be produced.
   c. Who should have the goods and services produced.
   d. How much of these goods and services should be produced.
1.31 c
1.32 a
1.33 e
1.34 b
1.35 d
1.36 Teacher check
1.37 Teacher check

SELF TEST 1

1.01   a
1.02   a
1.03   d
1.04   b
1.05   d
1.06   b
1.07   d
1.08   d
1.09   c
1.010 c
1.011 true
1.012 false
1.013 true
1.014 false
1.015 free enterprise
1.016 consumers
1.017 goods
1.018 economics
1.019 needs
1.020 resources
1.021 cannot
1.022 economic
1.023 profit
1.024 a
1.025 b
1.026 b
1.027 a
1.028 b
1.029 Any order:
   a. What goods and services should be produced.
   b. How goods and services should be produced.
   c. Who should have the goods and services produced.
   d. How much of these goods and services should be produced.
1.030 Economics is the study of production, distribution, and consumption of wealth.
1.031 free enterprise
1.032 communism
1.033 supply
1.034 socialism

SECTION 2

2.1	the materials found in nature which people put to use
2.2	man-made resources
2.3	businessmen
2.4	producers
2.5	b
2.6	d
2.7	f
2.8	h
2.9	g
2.10	e
2.11	c
2.12	a
2.13	true
2.14	false
2.15	true
2.16	false
2.17	abstaining from consumption
2.18	capital goods
2.19	Example: It improves the quality of labor and it increases productivity.
2.20	d
2.21	c
2.22	b
2.23	e
2.24	a
2.25	true
2.26	false
2.27	false
2.28	true
2.29	true

2.30 prices for consumers rise
(competition is keen)
(producers must use resources efficiently)
(products must be improved)

2.31 (producers do not have to use resources efficiently)
(producers make large profits)
prices for consumers drop
(consumers' wants cannot be satisfied)

2.32 Teacher check

2.33 Competition

2.34 economic

2.35 capitalists

2.36 government

2.37
a. _X_
b. ___
c. ___
d. _X_
e. ___
f. _X_

2.38 Any order:
a. regulates by making rules for effective operation
b. collects taxes
c. balances total supply and demand

2.39 Any order:
a. acts as a medium of exchange
b. serves as a store of value
c. gives a measure of value

2.40 deposits

2.41 b

2.42 c

2.43 a

SELF TEST 2

2.01	wants
2.02	free enterprise
2.03	resources
2.04	consumption
2.05	competition
2.06	communism
2.07	money
2.08	reserves
2.09	c
2.010	e
2.011	g
2.012	i
2.013	j
2.014	a
2.015	h
2.016	f
2.017	d
2.018	b
2.019	c
2.020	c
2.021	b
2.022	b
2.023	c
2.024	a
2.025	a
2.026	b
2.027	c
2.028	a
2.029	b
2.030	a
2.031	c
2.032	d
2.033	a

2.034 Any order:
a. a medium of exchange
b. a measure of value
c. a store of value

2.035 Any order:
a. regulatory
b. collects taxes
c. balances total supply and demand

2.036 a. F
b. B
c. F
d. F
e. B

2.037 a. B
b. F
c. C
d. F
e. C

SECTION 3

3.1	needs
3.2	give

3.3 Any order:
a. being greedy
b. being stubborn
c. being hasty
d. debt

3.4 goals

3.5 Any one:
soda
birthday
card
lunch

3.6 ten percent

3.7 Any order:
a. immediate
b. intermediate
c. long-range

3.8 a. income
b. expenses

3.9 bank

3.10 Teacher check
Note to teacher:
Students have been studying wants and needs, the roles of consumers and producers in the economy, financial decisions, and budgeting. This passage of Scripture discusses the virtuous woman and how she manages her resources, including her time.

SELF TEST 3

3.01   poverty
3.02   scattereth
3.03   instruction
3.04   needs
3.05   servant
3.06   ten
3.07   expenses
3.08   dollars
3.09   saving
3.010   wants
3.011   producers
3.012   deposits
3.013   mass
3.014   true
3.015   false
3.016   false
3.017   true
3.018   false
3.019   false
3.020   true
3.021   true
3.022   false
3.023   true
3.024   false
3.025   true
3.026   b
3.027   c
3.028   a
3.029   b
3.030   c
3.031   a
3.032   a
3.033   b
3.034   c
3.035   a
3.036   d
3.037   b
3.038   c
3.039   b
3.040   a
3.041   c
3.042   b
3.043   c
3.044   d
3.045   c
3.046   a
3.047   a

LIFEPAC TEST

1. i
2. e
3. f
4. k
5. b
6. d
7. j
8. h
9. l
10. a
11. g
12. c
13. c
14. e
15. g
16. i
17. k
18. m
19. a
20. l
21. j
22. h
23. f
24. d
25. b
26. b
27. c
28. a
29. a
30. b
31. c
32. d
33. c
34. c
35. b
36. Any order:
    a. What goods and services should be produced.
    b. How goods and services should be produced.
    c. Who should have the goods and services produced.
    d. How much of these goods and services should be produced.

ALTERNATE LIFEPAC TEST

1. j
2. e
3. h
4. b
5. f
6. k
7. c
8. i
9. a
10. d
11. g
12. l
13. p
14. n
15. o
16. a
17. k
18. b
19. d
20. c
21. e
22. i
23. j
24. f
25. h
26. d
27. c
28. d
29. a
30. c
31. d
32. b
33. d
34. c
35. a
36. consumer
37. rise
    or get higher
38. distributed
39. consumer
40. wants
41. Any order:
    a. wage controls
    b. price controls
    c. profit-making is forbidden
    d. government owns resources
    e. government determines production (allow additional answer if valid)

42.   a. production
          b. distribution
          c. consumption
43.   He will supply our needs.
44.   Any order:
          a. greed
          b. laziness
          c. haste
          d. debt

HISTORY & GEOGRAPHY 707

ALTERNATE LIFEPAC TEST

NAME _____

DATE _____

SCORE _____

78 / 98

Match these items (each answer, 2 points).

1. _____ free enterprise system
2. _____ consumption
3. _____ simple society
4. _____ capital
5. _____ economics
6. _____ tithe
7. _____ agrarian
8. _____ financial goals
9. _____ market
10. _____ barter
11. _____ communism
12. _____ production
13. _____ resources
14. _____ complex society
15. _____ subsidy

a. willingness to pay for goods or services

b. money or other resources available for investment

c. related to agriculture

d. trading goods or services for other goods or services

e. use of goods

f. study of production, distribution, and consumption of wealth

g. complete government control of production, distribution, and wages

h. system in which an individual or their close associates supply their own needs

i. immediate, intermediate, and long-term priorities for spending

j. private ownership of business with little government control

k. share of income devoted to the Lord's work

l. creation of goods to satisfy wants and needs

m. credit system

n. system in which individuals are highly dependent on each other economically

o. payment by government

p. all things available to satisfy wants or needs

Match these items (each answer, 2 points).

16. _____ budget
17. _____ choice
18. _____ labor force
19. _____ distribution
20. _____ monopoly
21. _____ competition
22. _____ division of labor
23. _____ investment
24. _____ supply
25. _____ demand

a. plan for spending and saving
b. working population
c. control of a resource or service by a single individual or corporation
d. transportation and sale of goods
e. attempt to sell by offering best goods at best price
f. amount of goods available
g. a form of taxation
h. demand for a commodity or service
i. assigning part of a production to different individuals
j. spending money on capital goods
k. determines which wants and needs will be met with ever-scarce resources

Write the letter for the correct answer on each line (each answer, 2 points).

26. Money can be used _____ .
    a. as a medium of exchange
    b. as a measure of value of goods and services
    c. as a way to store value; a mechanism for saving
    d. for all of the above

27. Our government gets money to finance needed public services through _____ .
    a. selling goods
    b. barter with other countries
    c. taxation
    d. confiscating private property

28. One book of the Bible which contains much good advice about money matters is _____ .
    a. Genesis   b. Revelation   c. Matthew   d. Proverbs

29. Money is commonly used as a medium of exchange, replacing barter, because _____ .
    a. it is more convenient
    b. the Bible condemns barter
    c. barter is illegal in the United States
    d. people can be cheated in barter

30. All of the following items are examples of ways governments might regulate economies
    except _____ .
    a. raising or lowering income taxes
    b. raising the interest on government bonds to encourage saving
    c. increasing the wants of citizens
    d. controlling prices on goods and services

31. When expenses threaten to exceed income, a budget planner should _____ .
    a. find a way to reduce expenses
    b. find a way to increase income
    c. re-examine goals and priorities
    d. consider various combinations of all of the above

32. Savings for a college education, retirement, or the purchase of a home are examples of
    _____ .
    a. immediate financial goals   b. long-term financial goals
    c. intermediate financial goals   d. foolish extravagance

33. Today's food purchases, buying a newspaper, and paying for a game ticket are examples
    of spending for _____ .
    a. basic needs   b. long-term financial goals
    c. intermediate goals   d. immediate goals

34. Banks can lend only as much money as _____ .
    a. borrowers ask to borrow
    b. their officers feel like lending
    c. they have back-up deposits in the Federal Reserve system
    d. they have on hand in the cashier's cages

35. The term *saving* in economics means _____ .
    a. postponing or abstaining from consumption
    b. reducing income
    c. spending money only for important things
    d. not needing or wanting anything that cost money

Complete the following statements (each answer, 3 points).

36.   Under a free enterprise system, production is really determined by what the
_____ wants and is willing to pay for.

37.   When demand is greater then supply, prices will usually _____ .

38.   Goods that have been produced must also be _____ to consumers,
which adds to the cost.

39.   Wages paid for a given job depend on its value to the ultimate _____
as well as on the number of workers available.

40.   Needs are those things necessary to sustain life; _____ are those things
people desire to have in addition.

Answer the following questions (each answer, 1 point).

41.   What are five economic controls which communist governments exert over their citizens?

   a. _____

   b. _____

   c. _____

   d. _____

   e. _____

42.   What are three things one learns about wealth in studying economics?

   a. _____

   b. _____

   c. _____

43.   What does God promise us concerning material needs?

   _____

44.   What are four things God cautions Christians to avoid in dealing with their financial affairs?

   a. _____

   b. _____

   c. _____

   d. _____

HISTORY & GEOGRAPHY 708

Unit 8: Political Science

TEACHER NOTES

MATERIALS NEEDED FOR LIFEPAC	
Required	Suggested
None	• examples of logical puzzles, optical illusions, and riddles • Bible • encyclopedia • current newspaper, news magazines, and atlases • reference books or online sources

ADDITIONAL LEARNING ACTIVITIES

Section 1: What Political Science Is

1. Conduct a class discussion about beliefs and knowledge. Select several commonly accepted beliefs, such as "children usually look and act like their parents," or "the world is round," and have class analyze the basis for each.

2. Have the class list and discuss examples of personal beliefs which are based on faith and personal feeling rather than sensory evidence or logical thought.

3. Tell students to imagine that the class is marooned on a tropical island, where no other humans are, although food is abundant. As a class, discuss what problems you would have to solve, and try to develop a scheme of government which would be fair to all. Draw a simple chart of that government. Explain that this activity was a simple example of what the early Pilgrims and pioneers faced in establishing homes in America.

4. Tell students to ask a science teacher or a college student majoring in science to explain to the class what the scientific method is and how a scientist would attack a problem such as testing a new medical procedure or a way of controlling harmful insects. This activity is an example of empirical thinking applied to a specific problem.

5. Have students list five common superstitions and ask several people whether they believe them and act upon them. How do you think each belief started? Have students write a brief summary of their results.

6. Instruct students to consult library references or online sources for information about an important discovery man has made, such as discovering electricity, how blood circulates, or the use of serums to fight disease. Then, assign them to write a brief report in which they decide whether the discovery resulted from logical thought, empirical evidence, faith, or a combination of these.

Section 2: Roots of Western Political Thought

1. Take a modern issue, such as capital punishment, control of air pollution, or voting rights for all. Have the class analyze how this issue would have been regarded by the various philosophers and schools of thought represented in this section.

2. Give examples of civil disobedience based on personal belief, such as Thoreau, Joan of Arc, or current protest groups. Discuss the idea of examining civil matters in the light of one's belief.

3. Arrange a visit to a Jewish synagogue (after communicating your purpose) or arrange for a speaker to explain the various rituals, traditions, and symbols of the Jewish religion.

4. Have a "Greek" day. Have each member of the class responsible for a picture, interesting fact, or quotation that will help them understand daily life and thought in ancient Greece.

5. Have students investigate the part that women played in the society and government of ancient Israel, early Greece, Rome, or early Christian groups.

Section 3: Modern Political Science

1. Assign students to write a report on one of the individuals mentioned in this section, such as Machiavelli or Thomas Jefferson. The report should include how the chosen person arrived at his main ideas.

2. Take several stories of government actions from one day's news. Include local and state governments as well as national. Have the class analyze the inputs and outputs that are detailed in each story.

3. Examine with the class symbols commonly used today by our government to keep citizens happy or to demonstrate interest in the citizens. Include military decorations, government-sponsored organizations and betterment programs, celebrations like the Bicentennial, flags, patriotic songs, the Statue of Liberty, and the national bird. Use pictures and records as well as discussion to evaluate these things.

4. Arrange for students to attend a city council meeting, a school board meeting, or a government-held public hearing (confirm that this is allowed). Have students analyze what they observe in terms of inputs and outputs, and predict the outcome if no decision is reached.

5. If your school has a student government, have the class draw a model of how it functions (for future use of your class or others).

6. Assign students to write a 250-word paper in which they summarize their own physical, social, and political environment.

7. Have students write a letter or an email to their own congressman either in support of some action they have taken or statement they have made, or as a request for action. Remind students to use accurate information and a formal, courteous tone. An adult should review the letter before it is sent.

Administer the LIFEPAC Test

The test is to be administered in one session. Give no help except with directions.
Evaluate the tests and review areas where the students have done poorly.
Review the pages and activities that stress the concepts tested.
If necessary, administer the Alternate LIFEPAC Test.

» ADDITIONAL ACTIVITY

The answer key on the following page applies to the additional activity.

» ADDITIONAL ACTIVITY ANSWER KEY

D
K
L

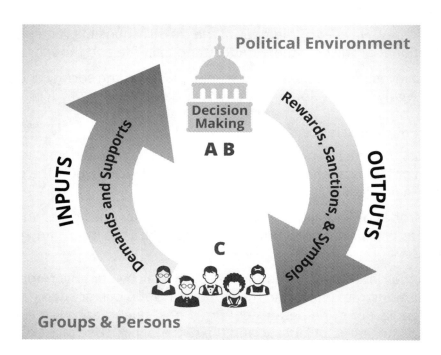

E
F
G
H
I
J
M

The additional activity on the following page may be reproduced as a student worksheet.

» ADDITIONAL ACTIVITY

Is it a group or an action?

This illustration is a model of a city government. Below the drawing are listed groups and actions concerned with a recent flood crisis. By using the letters for each item, place them on the diagram.

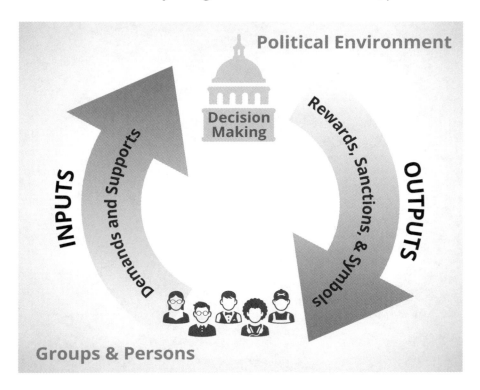

A. city council

B. city officials (police, judges)

C. citizens

D. citizens write letters requesting flood control and repairs

E. city council votes to repair flood-damaged streets and bridges

F. police judge gives looters stiff jail sentences

G. city council awards medal to boy who saved two children during flood

H. city council obtains Disaster Relief Funds for citizens from federal government

I. city erects monument to flood victims

J. future building in the flood area is prohibited by council

K. letters from several citizens thanking police for prompt action in disaster area appear in local news

L. mayor is re-elected soon after flood

M. city establishes flood-warning system

ANSWER KEYS

SECTION 1

1.1 ACROSS
1. theorist
2. rationalism
3. allocation
4. empiricism

DOWN
5. politics
6. fideism
7. epistemology

1.2 Either order:
a. leaders
b. laws

1.3 politics

1.4 Either order:
a. religious
b. philosophical

1.5 Either order:
a. political theory
b. epistemology

1.6 nations

1.7 behavior

1.8 opinions

1.9 Epistemology

1.10 evidence

1.11 true

1.12 true

1.13 false

1.14 false

1.15 false

1.16 true

1.17 mind

1.18 Nicolaus Copernicus

1.19 a. mathematics *or* rationalism
b. reasoning
c. center

1.20 knowledge

1.21 Teacher check

1.22 F, R

1.23 E

1.24 R

1.25 E

1.26 F

1.27 E, R

1.28 F

1.29 E, R

1.30 R

SELF TEST 1

1.01 Either order:
a. leaders
b. laws

1.02 Either order:
a. religious
b. philosophical

1.03 a. laws
b. government

1.04 politics

1.05 empirical

1.06 political

1.07 d

1.08 b

1.09 b

1.010 c

1.011 d

1.012 b

1.013 c

1.014 a

1.015 c

1.016 false

1.017 true

1.018 false

1.019 true

1.020 true

1.021 false

1.022 false

1.023 true

1.024 false

1.025 rationalism

1.026 Empiricism

1.027 faith

SECTION 2

2.1   ACROSS
   1. anarchy
   2. oligarchy
   3. Mosaic Code
   DOWN
   1. aristocracy
   2. republic
   3. hierarchy
   4. franchise
   5. cyclical

2.2   a. 600,000
   b. Moses

2.3   Pharaoh

2.4   anarchy

2.5   hierarchy

2.6   c

2.7   i

2.8   j

2.9   h

2.10   b

2.11   d

2.12   k

2.13   g

2.14   f

2.15   Look for the following:
   a. that the law was based on God's law and is unchanging
   b. that there is a brotherhood of man bound by the same law
   c. that laws for man could exist without the state and are not bound by the wishes of rulers

2.16   Look for the following:
   a. in man's relationship with his nation
   b. in man's relationship with other men
   c. man's relationship with his leaders

2.17   Hammurabi

2.18   God

2.19   false

2.20   false

2.21   true

2.22   false

2.23   true

2.24   false

2.25   Teacher check

2.26   true

2.27   false

2.28   true

2.29   false

2.30   true

2.31   false

2.32   true

2.33   Teacher check

2.34   The following items should be checked:
   ✓ One event that could never be repeated was the birth of Christ.
   ✓ The fall of Rome was not vital to Christianity.
   ✓ The best possible reflection of the City of God was the church.
   ✓ Man "lives" in two cities—that of God and that of earth.

2.35   false

2.36   true

2.37   false

2.38   true

2.39   true

2.40   true

2.41   true

2.42   true

2.43   b

2.44   b

2.45   b

2.46   d

2.47   d

2.48   Any order:
   a. Man is always free in his soul.
   b. All men must obey their rulers to be able to safely live together.
   c. Rulers only rule over a person's physical body.
   d. Nations exist to allow men to live together.

2.49   Teacher check

SELF TEST 2

2.01   ACROSS
    1. Augustus
    2. republic
    3. Hammurabi
    4. Visigoths
    5. Augustine
    6. Aristotle
    7. Copernicus
    8. Tarquin

    DOWN
    1. anarchy
    2. Plato
    3. oligarchy

2.02   cyclical

2.03   Christ

2.04   a. rise
    b. earthly

2.05   a. God
    b. earthly

2.06   Dark

2.07   Either order:
    a. Augustine
    b. Aristotle

2.08   soul

2.09   Either order:
    a. justice
    b. liberty

2.010 b

2.011 d

2.012 f

2.013 h

2.014 g

2.015 e

2.016 c

2.017 a

2.018 Any order:
    a. God's law is valid for all men.
    b. Law based on God's law does not change.
    c. Law can exist without any government when it comes from God.

2.019 Any order:
    a. Government comes from the minds of men.
    b. Democracy as a form of government.
    c. States can be divided into three groups based upon how many people rule: one, few, or many.

SECTION 3

3.1   Teacher check

3.2   power

3.3   a. authoritarian
    b. empirical thought *or* empiricism

3.4   leviathan

3.5   state of nature

3.6   evil nature

3.7   absolute

3.8   Either order:
    a. the right to demand protection against other men
    b. the right to self-defense

3.9   Either order:
    a. to gain power
    b. to gain prestige

3.10 c

3.11 b

3.12 a

3.13 d

3.14 a

3.15 Helper check

3.16 Thomas Jefferson

3.17 Either order:
    a. Hobbes
    b. Locke

3.18 a. George
    b. wrong

3.19 a. pilgrims
    b. compacts

3.20 Any order:
    a. social
    b. physical
    c. political

3.21 Greeks

3.22 majority

3.23 Any order:
    a. In the rule of one, all decisions are made at the top.
    b. In the rule of few, the decisions are made by consultation among the rulers.
    c. In the rule of many, citizens have a direct participation in the making of decisions.

3.24 c

3.25 a

3.26 b

3.27 *Supports* are inputs from the citizens that tell the decision makers in the government they are doing a good job. *Supports* can be votes, the payment of taxes, or even cheering when the leader of a group or nation rides in a parade.

Demands are inputs into the decision-making box that ask the decision makers to do something. Voting can be a *demand* if it is for the opposition party. It can also be a *support* if it is for the party in power.

3.28   I
3.29   I
3.30   O
3.31   I
3.32   O
3.33   O
3.34   O
3.35   I
3.36   Teacher check

SELF TEST 3

3.01   b
3.02   d
3.03   f
3.04   h
3.05   j
3.06   k
3.07   l
3.08   i
3.09   a
3.010 g
3.011 e
3.012 c
3.013 4
3.014 5
3.015 7
3.016 1
3.017 3
3.018 8
3.019 6
3.020 2
3.021 b
3.022 d
3.023 f
3.024 g
3.025 e
3.026 c
3.027 a
3.028 h
3.029 b
3.030 d
3.031 c
3.032 true
3.033 true
3.034 false
3.035 true
3.036 true
3.037 false
3.038 true
3.039 true
3.040 true
3.041 false
3.042 true
3.043 empirical
3.044 theorist
3.045 epistemology
3.046 logical
3.047 Any order:
    a. God's law does not change.
    b. God's law is valid for all men.
    c. God's law can exist without a particular government form.

LIFEPAC TEST

1. c
2. e
3. g
4. i
5. a
6. h
7. f
8. d
9. b
10. b
11. d
12. f
13. h
14. i
15. g
16. e
17. c
18. a
19. Machiavelli
20. Thomas Hobbes
21. a. birth
    b. Christ
22. liberty
23. rules
24. John Locke
25. false
26. false
27. true
28. false
29. true
30. d
31. c
32. d
33. a
34. b
35. c
36. ___2___
37. ___1___
38. ___3___
39. ___6___
40. ___7___
41. ___5___
42. ___4___

ALTERNATE LIFEPAC TEST

1. i
2. j
3. g
4. m
5. o
6. c
7. k
8. h
9. n
10. e
11. a
12. f
13. r
14. q
15. p
16. l
17. s
18. t
19. Example:
    Description tells what is seen.
    Explanation tells why and predicts outcomes.
20. Example:
    to explain and predict group behavior
21. Example:
    a covenant with God, not dependent on
    rulers or physical location
22. Example:
    The spirit dwells in the city of God. Man also
    exists in the everyday world (city of man) and
    must obey its laws.
23. Example:
    stressed duty of citizen to state—all males had
    a vote
24. Examples; any order:
    a. political theory
    b. comparative government
25. false
26. true
27. false
28. true
29. false
30. c
31. b
32. c
33. a
34. c
35. d

36. _J_
37. _G_
38. _C_
39. _C_
40. _G_
41. _J_
42. _C_
43. Any order:
    a. social
    b. physical
    c. political
44. Any three:
    a. parades
    b. speeches
    c. prizes
    or medals, honor, and so forth

HISTORY & GEOGRAPHY 708

ALTERNATE LIFEPAC TEST

NAME _____

DATE _____

SCORE _____

87 / 109

Match these items (each answer, 2 points).

1. _____ Moses
2. _____ model
3. _____ sanction
4. _____ Machiavelli
5. _____ Thomas Jefferson
6. _____ political science
7. _____ empirical evidence
8. _____ oligarchy
9. _____ Aristotle
10. _____ Augustine
11. _____ fideism
12. _____ epistemology
13. _____ Thomas Aquinas
14. _____ Thomas Hobbes
15. _____ symbol
16. _____ inputs
17. _____ politics
18. _____ rationalism

a. knowledge based on faith or personal feeling
b. republic
c. study of "who gets what, when, and how"
d. hierarchy
e. believed history is like a stream flowing toward the kingdom of God
f. study of how we know
g. a punishment or deterrent
h. rule of a society by a few people only
i. brought God's law to the Jewish people
j. a device for explaining and studying political systems or activities and predicting outcomes
k. observations made through the senses
l. demands and supports
m. author of a political book, *The Prince*
n. believed in rule by law, not men
o. wrote the Declaration of Independence
p. something designed to please citizens without actually solving problems
q. believed governments exist to control the evil in man
r. believed man's soul is always free
s. the making and administering of laws
t. emphasis on logical thought rather than senses or faith

Answer the following questions (each numbered item, 4 points).

19. What is the difference between description and explanation in political science?

_____

_____

_____

20. What is the goal of political science?

_____

_____

21. In what way was Jewish law different from that of other countries?

_____

_____

22. Augustine said that all men dwell in two "cities" at once. What did he mean?

_____

_____

_____

23. What was democratic government like in early Greece?

_____

_____

24. One area of study for political science is epistemology. What are the other two main areas?

a. _____   b. _____

Answer *true* **or** *false* (each answer, 1 point).

25. _____ Epistemology is the name for political parties in Greece.

26. _____ Machiavelli believed the chief purpose of any government was to increase its own power and prestige in the world.

27. _____ Jewish law was not concerned with man's relation to his fellows.

28. _____ Thomas Aquinas believed men should obey God's law, even if it was in conflict with man's law.

29. _____ A democratic society does not require any decision makers.

Write the letter for the correct answer on each line (each answer, 2 points).

30. Outputs (communications from rulers to people) include _____ .
    a. demands and supports
    b. manufactured goods
    c. rewards and sanctions
    d. tax payments

31. When citizens are in favor of what the government is already doing and vote to continue it, this input is called _____ .
    a. a demand
    b. a support
    c. a symbol
    d. an endorsement

32. In constructing models, the modern political scientists can use the _____ .
    a. newspaper ad
    b. printing machine
    c. computer
    d. television station

33. The Greek philosopher who stressed the rule of law over the changing opinions of men was _____ .
    a. Aristotle
    b. Plato
    c. Machiavelli
    d. Galileo

34. A political thinker much concerned about the rights of minorities was _____ .
    a. Thomas Hobbes
    b. Augustine
    c. John Stuart Mill
    d. Plato

35. A system or society in which no real leadership or established law exists is _____ .
    a. oligarchy
    b. hierarchy
    c. democracy
    d. anarchy

Write _J_ to indicate early Jewish society, _G_ for Greek society, and _C_ for early Christian society (each answer, 2 points).

36. _____ Mosaic Code

37. _____ simple democracy

38. _____ Thomas Aquinas

39. _____ outlived the fall of Rome in Europe

40. _____ Plato

41. _____ first considered moral laws were to be applied to all men

42. _____ City of God

Complete the following lists (each answer, 3 points).

43. List the three environments in which humans always live.

a. _____

b. _____

c. _____

44. List three examples of political symbols.

a. _____

b. _____

c. _____

HISTORY & GEOGRAPHY 709

Unit 9: State Economics and Politics

TEACHER NOTES

MATERIALS NEEDED FOR LIFEPAC	
Required	Suggested
None	• reference books or online sources

ADDITIONAL LEARNING ACTIVITIES

Section 1: State Government

1. Outline for the class the four levels of government—federal, state, county, and city. Discuss areas of responsibility and possible areas of confusion and conflict.

2. Be sure the class understands the difference between the three functions of government—legislative, administrative, and judicial. Point out that these functions are carried on at all levels of government.

3. As a class, make a wall chart of the departments of city, county, or state government and any federal agencies that have offices in your town. Put those that have similar functions together.

4. If possible, have the class visit your state legislature while it is in session. If not, invite one of your legislators or his assistant to talk to your class about the legislative process.

5. If your legislature is in session, have students follow the progress of one bill, in which they are interested, through the legislative procedure. Have students report on the outcome.

6. Have students find out about the career of your present state governor, and report to the class.

7. Have students make a graph showing the percentage of your state's taxes that are spent for these purposes: education, welfare, highways and bridges, state parks and recreation, and conservation.

8. Tell students to look at the Governments of States chart and make a chart for your state. The chart should show the elective offices and the names of the present officeholders.

Section 2: State Finance

1. Be sure class members understand that bonds are merely a form of borrowing money from investors, and that interest as well as principal must be paid back from future tax revenues. Use specific local examples and have students estimate cost of repayment, including interest.

2. Summarize your own state's tax revenues, and with the class's help classify them as regressive or progressive in nature.

3. Provide examples of specific shared-revenue programs. Discuss the effects on your state.

4. Assume that your state must raise additional taxes for $1 million to meet expenses. Divide the class into six groups; each group will discuss the advisability of one of the measures listed below. Have groups report their conclusions, and then have a class vote on the measure that is most preferred.

   a. Raise the present excise taxes on gasoline two cents per gallon.

   b. Charge a severance tax on the most valuable resource.

   c. Impose a 10% income tax on all incomes.

   d. Impose a sales tax or add to an existing sales tax.

   e. Raise taxes on real estate.

   f. Raise the present tax on inheritances.

5. Have students develop a simple quiz about taxation and administer it to at least twenty adults. Have the class tabulate the results and try to draw conclusions.

6. Help students find out what bond issues your state government now has outstanding. How does the total amount compare to the state's income?

7. If your state has an income tax, have the class find out how much a typical family pays.

8. If your state does not have an income tax, have the class figure out what other taxes raise the money needed for operation.

Section 3: State Politics

1. Arrange for a local precinct committee person or someone actively engaged in party political activities to discuss the procedures used in electing candidates.

2. Discuss the Christian's responsibilities in politics, both as a voter and a possible candidate.

3. Obtain copies of the most recent major party platforms and have the class compare them on several important issues.

4. If it is near election time, try to arrange a visit to a rally for one or more candidates. Observe how candidates appeal to voters and what various party workers do to promote each candidate's cause.

5. Divide the class into two groups, one representing liberal views and one conservative. Then, discuss this question as a class, using arguments you think each group might use: Should taxes be increased to provide better health care for all state citizens?

6. Assign students to report to class on one of these topics, including its history:

   a. Tammy Hall

   b. secret ballot

   c. gerrymandering

   d. ward bosses

   e. initiative and referendum

   f. the spoils system

   g. governors who have become presidents

7. Have students write a letter or an email to one of your state representatives in the legislature about a matter of concern. Make sure the topic is within the control of the state legislature. Parents should check over the letter, and revise if needed, before it is sent.
If students receive a reply, have them share it with the class.

8. Assign students to make a report on how statehood was achieved for your state and events of the early years of statehood.

Administer the LIFEPAC Test

The test is to be administered in one session. Give no help except with directions.
Evaluate the tests and review areas where the students have done poorly.
Review the pages and activities that stress the concepts tested.
If necessary, administer the Alternate LIFEPAC Test.

» ADDITIONAL ACTIVITY

The additional activity on the following page may be reproduced as a student worksheet.

» ADDITIONAL ACTIVITY ANSWER KEY

Who's in charge?

Federal Government	State Government	County or City Government
1, 2, 4, 5, 7, 8, 10, 13, 15, 16	6, 9, 11, 14, 17, 18	3, 12

» ADDITIONAL ACTIVITY

Who's in charge?

The following list gives a number of tasks of government. Put the identifying number in the column under the type of government that you think has this authority.

1. grants citizenship to new Americans
2. approves or disapproves people elected to congress
3. enforces dog leash laws
4. defends the country from outside invaders
5. makes treaties with other countries
6. decides who is eligible to vote in elections
7. maintains national parks and monuments
8. issues money
9. tries and sentences criminals who commit murder, robbery, and assault
10. settles arguments between states
11. settles arguments between neighboring towns
12. maintains city streets
13. builds national highways
14. checks records of states and counties (auditing)
15. greets ambassadors from other countries
16. regulates interstate commerce
17. licenses professionals such as lawyers, doctors, beauticians, and so forth
18. sets the standards for marriage licenses and ground for divorce

Federal Government	State Government	County or City Government

ANSWER KEYS

SECTION 1

1.1	f			

1.1 f
1.2 b
1.3 a
1.4 d
1.5 e
1.6 c
1.7 d
1.8 b
1.9 b
1.10 a
1.11 c
1.12 b
1.13 a
1.14 c
1.15 c
1.16 b
1.17 a
1.18 d
1.19 b
1.20 c
1.21 d
1.22 b
1.23 b
1.24 fifty
1.25 Either order:
    a. the U.S. government derives its authority from the states
    b. state government creates all other levels of government
1.26 Any order:
    a. legislative
    b. judicial
    c. executive
1.27 check and balance each other
1.28 "All power tends to corrupt and absolute power corrupts absolutely."
1.29 a. Montesquieu
    b. Spirit
    c. Laws
1.30 A legislature with one house is called unicameral while a legislature with two houses is called bicameral.
1.31 Either order:
    a. Senate
    b. House of Representatives
1.32 a. speaker
    b. lieutenant governor
1.33 population

1.34 a. over-represented
    b. under-represented
1.35 two
1.36 conservatives
1.37 a. speaker
    b. house
1.38 three
1.39 Nebraska
1.40 conservatives
1.41 majority
1.42 a. House
    b. Senate
1.43 special
1.44 minority
1.45 lobbyists
1.46 special interest
1.47 a. The bill is introduced.
    b. The bill is assigned a number and given to a committee in the house.
    c. The bill is considered by the committee.
    d. The bill is rejected by House committee or sent to the floor for approval.
    e. The bill is argued and voted in the House.
    f. The bill is considered by committee and then the full house in the Senate.
    g. The bill is sent to a conference committee with representatives of both houses.
    h. The bill from conference committee is voted on by both houses.
    i. The Governor signs or vetoes the bill.
    j. Legislature can override a veto.
1.48 executive
1.49 governor
1.50 a. strong
    b. weak
1.51 long
1.52 lieutenant governor
1.53 elected
1.54 freedom
1.55 administration
1.56 a. check
    b. balance
1.57 police
1.58 civil
1.59 a. budget
    b. vetoes
1.60 item
1.61 special session

1.62 pardons
1.63 leader
1.64 welfare
1.65 lawyer
1.66 attorney general
1.67 auditor
1.68 instruction
1.69 treasurer
1.70 f
1.71 c
1.72 a
1.73 b
1.74 e

SELF TEST 1

1.01 state
1.02 treaty
1.03 a. Constitution
     b. strengthen
1.04 revise
1.05 derived
1.06 independent
1.07 New England
1.08 interposition
1.09 Civil War
1.010 judicial
1.011 governor
1.012 judicial
1.013 power
1.014 Montesquieu
1.015 unicameral
1.016 false
1.017 true
1.018 false
1.019 true
1.020 false
1.021 true
1.022 true
1.023 true
1.024 false
1.025 false
1.026 true
1.027 true
1.028 true
1.029 g
1.030 a
1.031 e
1.032 b
1.033 j
1.034 i
1.035 k
1.036 c
1.037 f
1.038 d

SECTION 2

2.1   a. California
        b. New York
2.2   also rises
2.3   matched
2.4   welfare
2.5   education
2.6   inflation
2.7   governor
2.8   legislature
2.9   consumer
2.10   conservation
2.11   assessed
2.12   market
2.13   tax
2.14   California
2.15   local
2.16   education
2.17   God
2.18   protector
2.19   yes
2.20   "Render to Caesar the things that are Caesar's and to God the things that are God's..."
2.21   b
2.22   d
2.23   a
2.24   c
2.25   d
2.26   a
2.27   c
2.28   a
2.29   b
2.30   b
2.31   b
2.32   a
2.33   b
2.34   Long-term
2.35   bond
2.36   short
2.37   Revenue
2.38   Any order:
        a. serial
        b. general obligation
        c. revenue
2.39   Teacher check

SELF TEST 2

2.01   f
2.02   j
2.03   i
2.04   g
2.05   a
2.06   d
2.07   b
2.08   k
2.09   c
2.010   e
2.011   b
2.012   a
2.013   c
2.014   a
2.015   b
2.016   b
2.017   b
2.018   a
2.019   c
2.020   a
2.021   sovereignty
2.022   force
2.023   God
2.024   tax
2.025   Caesar's
2.026   income
2.027   higher
2.028   regressive
2.029   incentive
2.030   sales
2.031   i
2.032   a
2.033   h
2.034   b
2.035   c
2.036   d
2.037   e
2.038   f
2.039   k
2.040   j

SECTION 3

3.1   ACROSS
1. humanist
2. mercantilism
3. platform

DOWN
4. inflation
5. precinct
6. primary

3.2   varies
3.3   a. Liberal
b. Conservative
3.4   Ross Perot
3.5   political party
3.6   England
3.7   a. Tories
b. Whigs
3.8   Tories
3.9   Tories
3.10 Hamilton
3.11 Democratic-Republican
3.12 Republican
3.13 Whig
3.14 a. Clay
b. Webster
3.15 Republican
3.16 a. Cleveland
b. Wilson
3.17 eight
3.18 Whigs
3.19 government
3.20 Any order:
a. precinct
b. county
c. state
d. national
3.21 precinct
3.22 primary
3.23 state
3.24 precinct
3.25 parties
3.26 primary
3.27 chairman
3.28 rump
3.29 Either order:
a. liberal
b. conservative

3.30 conservatives
3.31 liberals
3.32 a. Hamilton
b. Jefferson
3.33 liberals
3.34 government
3.35 Word of God
3.36 socialism
3.37 social
3.38 moderates
3.39 compromises
3.40 unique
3.41 power
3.42 Gospel
3.43 abuse
3.44 machine
3.45 Tammany
3.46 Rayburn
3.47 competition
3.48 Either order:
a. finance
b. business
3.49 AFL-CIO
3.50 money
3.51 reform

SELF TEST 3

3.01	d
3.02	g
3.03	f
3.04	h
3.05	b
3.06	i
3.07	e
3.08	c
3.09	k
3.010	a
3.011	a
3.012	c
3.013	a
3.014	c
3.015	c
3.016	c
3.017	a
3.018	b
3.019	a
3.020	b
3.021	primary
3.022	cross
3.023	rump
3.024	liberalism
3.025	government
3.026	free
3.027	regressive
3.028	pragmatism
3.029	power
3.030	machines

LIFEPAC TEST

1. j
2. f
3. d
4. b
5. e
6. k
7. i
8. g
9. h
10. a
11. power
12. income
13. match
14. lobbyist
15. district attorney
16. taxpayer
17. education
18. judicial
19. Democratic
20. conservation
21. true
22. false
23. false
24. true
25. true
26. false
27. true
28. false
29. false
30. true
31. a
32. a
33. d
34. d

ALTERNATE LIFEPAC TEST

1. f
2. c
3. b
4. i
5. a
6. k
7. d
8. g
9. e
10. h
11. lobbyist
12. cross ballot
13. pragmatist
14. Republican
15. Democratic
16. regressive
17. derived
18. political machine
19. legislative
20. inherent
21. true
22. false
23. true
24. false
25. false
26. false
27. true
28. true
29. true
30. true
31. c
32. d
33. b
34. b

HISTORY & GEOGRAPHY 709

ALTERNATE LIFEPAC TEST

NAME _____

DATE _____

SCORE _____

54

68

Match these items (each answer, 2 points).

1. _____ conservative
2. _____ liberal
3. _____ revenue sharing
4. _____ secession
5. _____ judicial branch
6. _____ Articles of Confederation
7. _____ executive branch
8. _____ severance taxes
9. _____ platform
10. _____ precinct

a. part of state government responsible for enforcing laws and penalizing lawbreakers

b. systems where funds for specific use are provided partly by state and partly by federal government

c. tends to vote for increased social programs and government control of many aspects of business

d. governor and other state officials who administer laws

e. principles or programs that a party or candidate favors or promises

f. tends to favor tight control of spending and little government control over business

g. taxes imposed when a natural resource is used or extracted

h. smallest political unit

i. a state leaves the Union

j. branch of state government that creates new laws

k. agreement between colonies that preceded the Constitution

Complete these sentences using words from this list (each answer, 3 points).

Whigs	political machine	progressive tax
Democratic	cross ballot	pragmatist
Republican	lobbyist	special interest group
regressive tax	derived	legislature
inherent		

11.   A person who is paid to influence legislators to support a particular program in called a

_____ .

12.   A state that allows voters to vote for any candidate regardless of his party has a

_____ system.

13.   "If it works, I'm all for it!" is the statement of a _____ .

14.   The United States party that has the most conservative viewpoint as a whole is the

_____ party.

15.   The political party that has been dominant in national politics for the past forty or fifty years

is the _____ party.

16.   A tax that cost rich and poor citizens the same dollar amount is called a

_____ tax.

17.   The principle that the federal power of government comes from the sovereign states is called

_____ sovereignty.

18.   A powerful group of politicians dedicated to electing and keeping in office their own group of

candidates is called a _____ .

19.   The branch of state government that passes new laws is called the _____

branch.

20.   The power of God, the eternal, supreme power in the universe, is referred to as

_____ sovereignty.

Answer *true* **or** *false* (each answer, 1 point).

21. _____ One important official of a political party is its state chairman.

22. _____ Inflation does not affect state budgets.

23. _____ Consumers ultimately pay for many of the taxes levied against business.

24. _____ The governor of a state cannot pardon a murderer.

25. _____ Christians who contribute to church projects should not be expected to pay state taxes in addition.

26. _____ Payments for public welfare are very small in most states.

27. _____ Some state agencies become strong and, in effect, make laws.

28. _____ Licenses for drivers, fisherman, and so forth are one form of taxes.

29. _____ Two things states spend money on are highways and parks.

30. _____ The state auditor checks on the spending of all state departments.

Write the letter for the correct answer on each line (each answer, 2 points).

31. Groups of bonds issued by a state government to be paid off in yearly installments are called _____ .
    a. revenue bonds
    b. coupon bonds
    c. serial bonds
    d. savings bonds

32. A politician who favors much control by the federal government and high budgets for social programs is called a _____ .
    a. conservative
    b. Tory
    c. Dixiecrat
    d. liberal

33. A Christian must obey God's law, but also try to be a _____ .
    a. conservative
    b. law-abiding citizen
    c. pragmatist
    d. politician

34. A state that has a single "house" or lawmaking body in said to have a _____ legislature.
    a. unified
    b. unicameral
    c. whole
    d. federal

HISTORY & GEOGRAPHY 710

Unit 10: Social Sciences Review

TEACHER NOTES

MATERIALS NEEDED FOR LIFEPAC	
Required	Suggested
None	• world globe • wall maps (various projections): world, national, state, relief • simple pocket compass • reference books or online sources

ADDITIONAL LEARNING ACTIVITIES

Section 1: History and Geography

1. Discuss these questions with your class.

   a. Do the qualities of character required of the historian match the qualities of character required of the Christian?

   b. Give examples of the contributions of ancient civilizations that can be pointed out today in the classroom.

   c. In what way has God given us the total picture of history?

   d. Describe ways that local geography has affected the way of life here in our city (town, county, etc.).

2. Make maps as a class. Several students should work together to prepare simple but accurate maps of familiar landmarks, the school and campus, the church buildings and grounds, a nearby park or playground. Other groups of students may test the accuracy by following the maps.

3. Instruct students to research the compass with these directions: Find out what is meant by "boxing the compass." Be able to define *cardinal points* and *variation*. Explain how the mariner's compass differs from other types. Students can perform simple experiments for the rest of the class.

4. Have the class make a chronological chart of explorers of North America from 1000 A.D. through the 1600s. If time and resources permit, date may be extended to the 1800s, with each student taking a century or part of a century. The advantage of extending the time frame is that the student becomes aware of the relative newness of our country.

5. Have students research and report to the class on the life and contributions of an early map maker or explorer.

Section 2: Anthropology and Sociology

1. Discuss these questions with your class.

   a. Is it possible for a church to be a "primary group" for one person and a "secondary group" for another? Explain.

   b. Why is it important for the anthropologist and the sociologist to avoid bias and prejudice?

   c. What examples can you give of "social change" that you have observed in the last few months? In the last year? Since the Bicentennial?

   d. How did the environment of the Holy Land affect the culture of people living in Bible times?

2. Instruct partners to pretend that they are a team of archaeologists by "discovering" objects in the classroom and then "guessing" what their use might be.

3. Several students of similar national or ethnic background may describe to the class some of the foods, holidays, or traditions they and their families share.

4. Have students research a North American Native American tribe, and then tell the class how environment influenced tribal culture.

5. Assign students to research and report on a specific invention or discovery and the cultural change it brought about.

Section 3: Economics and Politics

1. Discuss these questions with your class.

   a. What do you think a "utopia," or idealized society, would be from a Christian viewpoint?

   b. Why do civilized societies need money?

   c. How are political candidates chosen?

   d. What is a "political platform"?

   e. Is "economics" something that affects only bankers and politicians?

   f. What factors (other than basic human needs) affect the way we spend our money?

2. Have students work out a model "budget" for a specific school or church project. They should include all costs, such as utilities and transportation. "Capital" may include tithes, donations, sales of goods or services, and grants. Have them present the budget to the rest of the class for approval or rejection.

3. Divide the class into two or more political parties. Each party should draw up a platform of proposals and present the platforms to the class for vote. Note: Students will enjoy a campaign based on ideals and principles rather than on personalities. However, elections may be held at the teacher's discretion.

4. Tell students to use a good Bible dictionary, concordance, or online resources to see what references they can find to money transactions in the Old Testament.

5. Have students research and describe to the class the position and function of the "money changer" in the New Testament.

6. Assign students to research and report to the class the life and contributions of one of the philosophers who influenced Western political thought.

7. Have the class draw a chart of your state government, indicating those officials who are elected and those who are appointed.

Administer the LIFEPAC Test

The test is to be administered in one session. Give no help except with directions.
Evaluate the tests and review areas where the students have done poorly.
Review the pages and activities that stress the concepts tested.
If necessary, administer the Alternate LIFEPAC Test.

ANSWER KEYS

SECTION 1

1.1 ACROSS
    1. historiography
    2. equinox
    3. sphere
    4. predecessors
    DOWN
    1. habitat
    2. solstice
    3. glacier
    4. Pilgrims
    5. foci
    6. estuary
    7. linear

1.2 b
1.3 d
1.4 f
1.5 h
1.6 j
1.7 k
1.8 i
1.9 g
1.10 e
1.11 c
1.12 a
1.13 a. God
    b. mankind
    c. his environment
1.14 Any three:
    a. social
    b. political
    c. racial
    or religious, economic, technological, cultural
1.15 Any order:
    a. ideas about law
    b. writing
    c. trade
    or farming, system of weights and measures, calendar
1.16 Either order:
    a. an alphabet
    b. the spread of civilization
1.17 Either order:
    a. information about the one true God
    b. the Old Testament literature and commandments
1.18 cyclical
1.19 linear
1.20 a. creation
    b. judgment

1.21 false
1.22 true
1.23 true
1.24 true
1.25 false
1.26 true
1.27 false
1.28 true
1.29 true
1.30 false
1.31 true
1.32 false
1.33 true
1.34 primary
1.35 secondary
1.36 a. archaeological
    b. written
1.37 Any order:
    a. accurate
    b. patient
    c. judgmental
    d. moral
    e. tenacious
1.38 Any order:
    a. books
    b. diaries
    c. magazines
    d. treaties
1.39 physical
1.40 a. meteorology
    b. climatology
1.41 twenty-four
1.42 Either order:
    a. east
    b. west
1.43 Either order:
    a. north
    b. south
1.44 a. twenty-four
    b. hour
1.45 c
1.46 e
1.47 l
1.48 g
1.49 i
1.50 a
1.51 f
1.52 b
1.53 k
1.54 d

1.55 Any four:
   a. climate
   b. industry
   c. earth's surface
   d. people
   or countries
      continents
      products
1.56 Any order:
   a. polar
   b. interrupted-area
   c. Mercator
1.57 Any order:
   a. Pacific
   b. Mountain
   c. Central
   d. Eastern
1.58 true
1.59 true
1.60 false
1.61 false
1.62 true
1.63 true
1.64 true
1.65 false
1.66 Any four:
   a. rivers
   b. plains
   c. valleys
   d. plateaus
   or mountains
      hills
      oceans
1.67 a. A triangular piece of land made by deposits of mud and sand at the mouth of a river.
   b. An area of ocean (salt water) partly surrounded by land.
   c. Vast expanse of relatively flat land.
   d. High, flat area of land.
1.68 seventy
1.69 a. Mississippi
   b. Nile
   c. Ganges
1.70 Any order:
   a. mining
   b. forestry
   c. grazing
1.71 Any order:
   a. North American
   b. Eurasian
   c. Amazon

1.72 false
1.73 false
1.74 true
1.75 true
1.76 true
1.77 a. northeast
   b. industrial
1.78 a. cold
   b. warm
1.79 Any order:
   a. Creeks
   b. Cherokee
   c. Choctaw
   d. Chickasaw
   e. Seminole
1.80 Spanish
1.81 a. M
   b. M
   c. W
   d. W
   e. S
   f. S
1.82 a. S
   b. W
   c. N
   d. W
   e. M
   f. N

SELF TEST 1

1.01   c
1.02   e
1.03   g
1.04   i
1.05   k
1.06   a
1.07   l
1.08   j
1.09   h
1.010 f
1.011 d
1.012 b
1.013 c
1.014 c
1.015 d
1.016 b
1.017 d
1.018 a. God
           b. man
           c. environment
1.019 physical
1.020 a. Spanish
           b. southern
1.021 seventy
1.022 God
1.023 true
1.024 false
1.025 true
1.026 true
1.027 true
1.028 true
1.029 true
1.030 false
1.031 false
1.032 Any order:
           a. Babylonians
           b. Phoenicians
           c. Egyptians
           d. Hebrews
1.033 a. Denali
           b. Death
           c. west
1.034 a. Revolutionary
           b. Industrial
1.035 true
1.036 true
1.037 true
1.038 true
1.039 true
1.040 true

SECTION 2

2.1   a
2.2   c
2.3   e
2.4   g
2.5   i
2.6   h
2.7   f
2.8   d
2.9   b
2.10   past
2.11   present
2.12   anthropology
2.13   Culture
2.14   language
2.15   false
2.16   true
2.17   true
2.18   false
2.19   true
2.20   false
2.21   true
2.22   true
2.23   false
2.24   true
2.25   ACROSS
           1. heterozygous
           2. monograph
           3. genealogical
           4. utopia
           5. immigrants
           6. nonliterate
           DOWN
           1. homozygous
           2. race
           3. genus
           4. valid
           5. function
           6. hypothesis
2.26   false
2.27   true
2.28   true
2.29   true
2.30   e
2.31   a, f
2.32   h
2.33   b
2.34   c
2.35   d, g

2.36	Either order:		**2.69**	ACROSS
	a. family			1. pastoralists
	b. church			2. emigrate
2.37	association			3. oracle
2.38	institution			4. artifact
2.39	a. primary			DOWN
	b. secondary			1. pueblo
2.40	acculturation			2. magic
2.41	assimilation			3. stereotype
2.42	true		**2.70**	e
2.43	false		**2.71**	b
2.44	true		**2.72**	a
2.45	false		**2.73**	c
2.46	true		**2.74**	d
2.47	true		**2.75**	f
2.48	Any order:		**2.76**	Either order:
	a. self-control			a. environment
	b. self-image			b. culture
	c. basic discipline		**2.77**	intermarriage
	d. knowledge of social roles		**2.78**	Any order:
2.49	Either order:			a. divination
	a. Adam			b. visions
	b. Eve			c. omens
2.50	earth			d. magic
2.51	206			e. oracles
2.52	language		**2.79**	magic
2.53	eternal		**2.80**	Native Americans
2.54	a. Homo		**2.81**	Any order:
	b. sapiens			a. style of shelter
2.55	Any order:			b. clothing
	a. a population			c. society
	b. a common language			d. food gathering technique
	c. an environment		**2.82**	melting
2.56	a. Japhetites		**2.83**	a. Bering Strait
	b. Semites			b. Asia
	c. Hamites		**2.84**	hunters
2.57	Any order:		**2.85**	cultures
	a. hair features		**2.86**	written
	b. height		**2.87**	sachems
	c. facial features		**2.88**	f, i, l
	d. skin color		**2.89**	e, j
2.58	a. Shem		**2.90**	g, h
	b. Ham		**2.91**	a
	c. Japeth		**2.92**	a, b
2.59	false		**2.93**	d, k
2.60	true		**2.94**	c
2.61	true		**2.95**	Any order:
2.62	true			a. Canada
2.63	true			b. Alaska
2.64	true		**2.96**	lamp
2.65	true		**2.97**	a. Tahiti
2.66	true			b. Marquesas
2.67	false			
2.68	false			

2.98 Examples:
— Inuits who lived near the sea fished or depended on seal for food.
— Inland Inuits hunted caribou for food and for skins and bones.
— Inuits who lived on the frozen Arctic Ocean built igloos out of hard snow, the most readily available material in the environment.
— Hunters used the skins of animals for clothing, shelter, and boats. Animals bones and horns were used for tools.

2.99 Any order:
a. political oppression
b. economic deprivation
c. religious persecution

2.100 prejudice
2.101 discrimination
2.102 g
2.103 e
2.104 f
2.105 a
2.106 h
2.107 b
2.108 d
2.109 c
2.110 Teacher check
2.111 culture
2.112 changes
2.113 language
2.114 false
2.115 true
2.116 Example:
A change in the family from extended families involved in interpersonal relationships with other members of the community to nuclear families that are generally isolated from their neighbors in terms of relationships.

SELF TEST 2

2.01 o
2.02 j
2.03 n
2.04 b
2.05 g
2.06 a
2.07 q
2.08 p
2.09 d
2.010 c
2.011 i
2.012 r
2.013 f
2.014 l
2.015 e
2.016 Archaeological
2.017 language
2.018 biased
2.019 a. Anthropology
b. geography
2.020 Any order:
a. religious
b. political
c. economic
2.021 environment
2.022 Iroquois
2.023 a. Hunter-gatherers
b. horticulturists
2.024 magic
2.025 Either order:
a. environment
b. culture
2.026 c
2.027 b
2.028 b
2.029 a
2.030 d
2.031 b
2.032 d
2.033 a
2.034 true
2.035 true
2.036 false
2.037 true
2.038 true
2.039 false
2.040 true
2.041 true
2.042 false
2.043 false

SECTION 3

3.1 ACROSS
  1. free enterprise
  2. agrarian
  3. confederacy
  4. competition
  5. capital
  DOWN
  2. empiricism
  3. candidate
  4. equitable
  5. pragmatism
  6. bicameral
  7. fideism
  8. consumer
  9. entrepreneur
  10. hierarchy
3.2 c
3.3 e
3.4 g
3.5 a
3.6 h
3.7 f
3.8 d
3.9 b
3.10 b
3.11 d
3.12 f
3.13 h
3.14 g
3.15 e
3.16 c
3.17 a
3.18 Any order:
  a. competition
  b. money
  c. the market
  d. government
3.19 a. production
  b. distribution
  c. consumption
3.20 Any order:
  a. food
  b. clothes
  c. shelter
3.21 farming
3.22 simple
3.23 complex

3.24 a
3.25 c
3.26 e
3.27 g
3.28 h
3.29 f
3.30 d
3.31 b
3.32 true
3.33 false
3.34 true
3.35 true
3.36 true
3.37 Examples:
  a. The government makes all production decisions, controls wages paid to workers, and owns all natural and capital resources.
  b. The government owns some things, such as railroads and heavy industries, but some industries are owned by private citizens.
3.38 Any order:
  a. medium of exchange
  b. measure of value
  c. store of value
3.39 a. manage
  b. debt
3.40 tax
3.41 education
3.42 legislation
3.43 a. property
  b. income
  c. sales
3.44 govern
3.45 government
3.46 governments
3.47 empiricism
3.48 rationalism
3.49 fideism
3.50 false
3.51 true
3.52 Any order:
  a. Jewish civilization
  b. Greek civilization
  c. Roman civilization
  or Christianity

3.53   c

3.54   e

3.55   g

3.56   i

3.57   k

3.58   a

3.59   j

3.60   h

3.61   f

3.62   d

3.63   b

3.64   false

3.65   true

3.66   true

3.67   true

3.68   true

3.69   false

3.70   false

3.71   Any order:
   a. God has granted equality to all men.
   b. All men have equal rights at birth.
   c. Human rights include life, liberty, and the pursuit of happiness.
   d. Human rights are self-evident.
   e. If a government abolishes human rights, the people can abolish that government.

3.72   state

3.73   Any order:
   a. legislative
   b. executive
   c. judicial

3.74   a. a loose association of states for a common purpose
   b. says that states may block the enforcement of a federal law
   c. a theory that a state may declare a federal law null and void
   d. is when a state leaves the Union

3.75   a. checks
   b. balances

3.76   a. bicameral
   b. unicameral

3.77   lobbyists

3.78   Examples:
   a. A strong governorship is one in which the governor appoints his own cabinet; almost all of the state administrators report to him.
   b. A weak governorship is one in which almost every major officeholder is elected. Elected officials have a sense of responsibility to the voters who elected them, rather than to the governor.

3.79   c

3.80   d

3.81   b

3.82   e

3.83   a

3.84   false

3.85   true

3.86   false

3.87   true

3.88   true

3.89   party

3.90   Either order:
   a. Republican
   b. Democratic

3.91   a. conservative
   b. liberal
   c. moderate

3.92   God's

SELF TEST 3

3.01	g		**3.047**	_4_
3.02	p		**3.048**	_6_
3.03	k		**3.049**	_2_
3.04	c		**3.050**	_5_
3.05	o		**3.051**	_1_
3.06	h		**3.052**	_3_
3.07	m		**3.053**	_7_
3.08	a			
3.09	f			
3.010	b			
3.011	l			
3.012	n			
3.013	e			
3.014	i			
3.015	d			
3.016	c			
3.017	d			
3.018	a			
3.019	c			
3.020	b			
3.021	b			
3.022	d			
3.023	a			
3.024	c			
3.025	map			
3.026	environment			
3.027	language			

3.028 Any order:
    a. religious
    b. political
    c. economic

3.029 a. checks
    b. balances

3.030	false
3.031	true
3.032	false
3.033	true
3.034	true
3.035	true
3.036	false
3.037	true
3.038	true
3.039	true
3.040	false
3.041	true
3.042	false
3.043	true
3.044	true
3.045	true
3.046	false

LIFEPAC TEST

1.	a	**47.**	farming
2.	c	**48.**	Aristotle
3.	e	**49.**	Any order:
4.	g		a. Hebrew
5.	i		b. Greek
6.	j		c. Roman
7.	h		
8.	f		
9.	d		
10.	b		
11.	b		
12.	c		
13.	d		
14.	c		
15.	a		
16.	d		
17.	i		
18.	j		
19.	g		
20.	e		
21.	c		
22.	a		
23.	b		
24.	d		
25.	f		
26.	h		
27.	true		
28.	false		
29.	false		
30.	false		
31.	false		
32.	true		
33.	true		
34.	true		
35.	false		
36.	b		
37.	d		
38.	f		
39.	g		
40.	e		
41.	c		
42.	a		

43. Any order:
a. economic
b. political
c. religious

44. Any one:
Scriptures
or Bible, Word of God

45. stereotyping

46. Empiricism

ALTERNATE LIFEPAC TEST

1. f
2. t
3. e
4. o
5. p
6. j
7. m
8. a
9. q
10. k
11. n
12. c
13. h
14. s
15. b
16. d
17. g
18. i
19. r
20. l
21. c
22. b
23. a
24. d
25. d
26. c
27. _6_
28. _1_
29. _4_
30. _3_
31. _7_
32. _2_
33. _5_
34. f
35. g
36. a
37. b
38. e
39. c
40. d
41. Example:
    tensions and anxieties
42. ethnocentrism
43. one hour
44. Example:
    God the Father before Creation
45. Example:
    all mankind

46. Examples:
    a. natural barriers
       unsuited for agriculture
       good for grazing
       hinder transportation
       lumber resources
       mineral deposits
    b. separate land masses
       affect climate
       used for transportation and trade
       provide fishing and shipping
    c. good for grazing
       hinder transportation
       scarce rainfall
    d. fertile soil
       support large populations
       good for trade and transportation
    e. poor soil
       good grazing

HISTORY & GEOGRAPHY 710

ALTERNATE LIFEPAC TEST

NAME _____

DATE _____

SCORE _____

94
118

Match these items (each answer, 1 point).

1. _____ Great Plains Indians
2. _____ Holy Scriptures
3. _____ Mercator
4. _____ Adam and Eve
5. _____ Babylonians
6. _____ positivism
7. _____ Five Civilized Tribes
8. _____ polar projection
9. _____ delta
10. _____ Mariana Trench
11. _____ equator
12. _____ culture
13. _____ Utopia
14. _____ Africans
15. _____ solstice
16. _____ equinox
17. _____ reliefs
18. _____ assimilation
19. _____ acculturation
20. _____ fideism

a. useful for mapping airline routes
b. occurs when sun is farthest north or farthest south
c. the ways in which man subdues his environment
d. occurs twice a year when nights everywhere are twelve hours long
e. especially useful when determining direction
f. became the stereotype of the North American Indian
g. geographical features
h. an idealized society
i. occurs when one culture is taken over by a more dominant culture
j. a way of knowing based on observed facts
k. lowest point on earth
l. a way of knowing based on an act of faith
m. Native American people who developed a written language and a code of laws
n. imaginary line around the center of the earth
o. the shared ancestors of all mankind
p. contributed a system of weight and measures
q. triangular piece of land at the mouth of a river
r. occurs when two societies interact by trading cultures
s. came to this country as slaves
t. gives the total picture of history
u. conservative political viewpoint

Write the letter for the correct answer on each line (each answer, 2 points).

21. Archaeological remains may contain _____ .
    a. letters and diaries
    b. old political machines
    c. pottery, tools, and bones
    d. books and newspapers

22. The dates assigned to earth and to its prehistoric remains are _____ .
    a. positively known
    b. only estimates
    c. forever constant
    d. always predictable

23. Societies in which people depend upon themselves and their immediate families to supply their needs are _____ .
    a. primitive
    b. socialist
    c. communist
    d. complex

24. The training a person receives so that they can function successfully in a society is _____ .
    a. cultural change
    b. civilization
    c. stability
    d. socialization

25. Noticeable areas of racial difference include _____ .
    a. facial features
    b. skin color and hair texture
    c. physical height
    d. a, b, and c

26. The most important single component of a shared culture is _____ .
    a. food, clothing, and shelter
    b. some way to foretell the future
    c. a common language
    d. socialization

Number these events in the proper order (each answer, 2 points).

27. _____ The governor may veto the bill or sign it into law.

28. _____ The bill is introduced, given a number, and assigned to a committee.

29. _____ The bill goes to a joint committee to resolve differences.

30. _____ The bill is sent to a committee of the other house and onto the floor for debate and approval.

31. _____ If the governor vetoes the bill, the legislature may override it by a two-thirds vote.

32. _____ The committee considers the bill and sends it to the floor for debate and approval.

33. _____ The bill goes back to both houses for approval and then is sent back to the governor.

Match these items (each answer, 2 points).

34. _____ system of courts and judges

35. _____ hills, plateaus, rivers, and deltas

36. _____ elected representatives and senators

37. _____ magic, divination, and oracles

38. _____ Native Americans, immigrants, and descendants of immigrants

39. _____ governor, lieutenant-governor, and Secretary of State

40. _____ socialism, communism, free enterprise

a. legislative branch

b. means of foretelling the future

c. executive branch

d. economic systems

e. population of the U.S.

f. judicial branch

g. landforms

h. political parties

Complete the following statements (each answer, 3 points).

41. Sudden cultural changes tend to cause _____ .

42. Concluding that a foreign culture is inferior to one's own culture is called

_____ .

43. Each of the world's twenty-four time zones represents _____ of time.

44. History began with _____ .

45. To fully understand the history of any one civilization or country one must study the history

of _____ .

Answer this question (each answer, 5 points).

46. What is one effect each landform may have on man's way of life?

a. mountains _____

_____

b. seas and oceans _____

_____

c. plateaus _____

_____

d. plains _____

_____

e. hills _____

_____